FORGING AF

Alf Strange and Dr. Margaret Simmons, F.R.C.P. (Consultant Physician).

By kind permission of the Shropshire Star.

FORGING AHEAD

Alf Strange

GEE AND SON, DENBIGH

First Impression: February 1994
Second Impression: April 1997

ISBN 0 7074 0240 9

By the same author:
'Me Dad's the Village Blacksmith'
'Following Me Dad'

Printed and Published by
GEE & SON (DENBIGH) LTD., DENBIGHSHIRE, WALES

Introduction

ALF STRANGE'S two previous books, *Me Dad's the Village Blcaksmith* and *Following Me Dad,* his third book entitled *Forging Ahead* is a must.

This book is about the later years of his life around his beloved village of Welsh Frankton. It starts about a sad story of his family and then goes on to tell us his experiences of his blacksmith business and farming. Included in these stories are when his cattle went down with the dreaded Foot and Mouth disease in his area, when thousands of cattle were destroyed. It was a very worrying time for myself because I had 150 cattle slaughtered in a single morning.

This and many other amusing stories of his sporting life are included and told in Alf's own words of country life in Shropshire.

I am honoured to be asked once again by Alf to write a few words about his latest book. I am quite sure that you will enjoy it and you will not put it down until you have read the last page.

GRAFTON BEDDOES

Acknowledgements

AGAIN I wish to record grateful thanks to my friend Bernard Hallett for all his help, and to Iorwerth Roberts for his invaluable assistance during the preparation of this book.

My sincere thanks are due once again to the publishers, Gee and Son (Denbigh) Ltd. for all their help and guidance.

Foreword

JUST a few thoughts on a wet day. Life is very short really. As a lad who has never been very far from his own village — as a teenager, I looked at men who would be in their forties. They were the 'men of the village' — helping out at garden fetes, dances in the parish hall. Men, one thought, could never be done without, an indispensible group.

Then, as I myself, reached thirty years of age, these men would be in their sixties. Looking at the minutes of certain village clubs, and societies, one sees that the majority had served on one committee or another.

Before very long, the age group passed on and I was an 'elder' of the village — making decisions on one committee or another. Suddenly it hits one — one's mates start to pass away — at the doctors one sees some old mates there too with various complaints that usually come with old age — pains in the chest, arthritis in the knees and hips, a bit of water trouble, dizziness if they rush about.

When sitting in the car on the streets of Ellesmere, you see someone you think you recognise but whom you have not seen for many years. 'No, it can't be!' you say, 'He has grey hair and walks on two sticks!' As he gets closer, you realise he is the someone against whom you played football or cricket in yester-year — a fast bowler, a centre-forward, a good runner or a good dart pitcher. You realise life has nearly gone full circle and that there is something one cannot do — turn the clock back.

How you wish you could have been as wise in your youth as you are now, and listened to your elders. But the old saying will never alter — there is no substitute for youth and there is no substitute for experience. How I wish now I could combine the two — which reminds me to a story of the man who had made money his God. All he had done in his life was to try to make more. He eventually passed away and someone asked the question : 'How much did he leave?' The answer was 'The Lot.'

There are two things to aim for in life —
Firstly to achieve what you have set out to do.
And secondly,
To enjoy what you have achieved.

Only the wisest of men manage the second. Life is not a dress rehearsal. It is the real show — so enjoy it.

'You can't put into someone what God has left out' . . .

Contents

List of Illustrations

Chapter 1

Unforgotten — 80 Years On

ON a wet July morning, I have found both the time and inclination to put pen to paper, at last to start my third book on village life and the characters I have known in my beloved village of Welsh Frankton. My first two covered from around 1870 to about 1950 — this one I intend to cover from 1950 possibly to the present day.

Before I record some anecdotes of this modern era, I feel I should hark back to an incident from earlier times, missed out of the first two books, as it really puts the present into its historical context.

It concerns the death of my Uncle Will (my mother's youngest brother) in Singapore in 1917 and a sequel that literally happened barely two months ago in 1992.

Will Ryder was called up for war service in the First World War. The K.S.L.I., together with his battalion, was posted to Singapore, en route to quell a melee in the Indian Army. Unfortunately, he caught malaria, and died, as did his mate. The usual telegram : 'I regret to inform you that your son, Private Will Ryder, has died whilst on active service' (one of thousands sent to homes in the United Kingdom in World War One, arrived in his home in Tetchill.

I have often thought in later years how cold and abrupt that sad message was. I often saw my Grannie Ryder shedding a tear, and my mother, too, when something cropped up about their son and brother Will. Over the years, as I walk past our village War Memorial, on which the names of fourteen lads of the village are inscribed (some with no known graves), of the heartbreak their untimely passing caused.

The reason I chose to start this third book with this story is an incident that happened less than two months ago. I read a cutting in the Shropshire Star :

'While on a visit to Singapore to commemorate the fall of Singapore in 1942 to the Japanese, at Kranje Memorial Cemetery, my son and I discovered the graves of three King's Shropshire Light Infantry buried during the period of the Great War 1914 - 1918 — details as follows :

Lieut. H. S. Elliot, 15th February 1915 age 25

Private W. H. Ryder, 3rd February 1917 age 23

Private A. Walker 15th April 1915 age 20.'

The letter goes on to say Mr. W. E. Foster of Oswestry wondered whether any of Will Ryder's relatives still lived in Shropshire. We contacted him that it was the grave of our dear Uncle Will, and he kindly sent up the photograph he took of the headstone on it. I know my granny and my mother would have loved to see that memorial and to know their son and brother has a resting place, be it in a foreign country.

As I write, I have before me a painting of Tetchill Moor House, the old family home of the Ryders. Will, a humble farm lad, painted aged 17. Its frame is tatty, the paint is discoloured, and in the corner are the words 'A Country Cottage — Who Knows Where?'.

Alf Ryder, Will's youngest brother (My Uncle Alf) who passed away in 1978, gave me the painting saying: 'I know you'll look at it often.' At the same time I was given the old family copper warming pan — it hangs still by the fireplace in our front room. The painting hangs up in my old railway container, which happens to be my registered office with the authorities in London. In the corner, I have placed the photographs of Uncle Will's grave sent me by Mr. Foster — somehow it seems apt that the two should be together.

It is just another story of village life, and events that happened so many years ago, but which in my opinion deserve to be recorded because they tell of the heartache and hardship of rural life in yesteryear and of a way of life that I am afraid has passed, never to return. The 1914 - 18 War was said to be the 'War to End All Wars' and still today, men cannot live in peace with one another. I am glad to have recorded that little story for future generations — but is it really nearly 80 years since it all happened?

Chapter 2

Horse to Tractor

IT is now almost 50 years since one of the worst winters that I remember for snow — 1947. It started snowing on Boxing Day, just as Frankton finished a football match on Hardwicke Park. We did not play there again until March because of the snow.

My mother had an operation in the old R.S.I. and was in for quite a while — 40 miles there and back. In those days, that was quite a journey. The Perthy Road was blocked to traffic for weeks and the main road to Ellesmere and Whittington had just four tracks. The snow was so deep and the cold winds had frozen it so hard that snow ploughs could not cope with it. The only way was with a pick and shovel, and what a long hard and tedious job that was!

Luckily the A5 from Whittington to Shrewsbury had been kept open. Today we pop to Shrewsbury in 20 minutes or less in our modern cars, but in those days, it was nothing to have radiators frozen solid as soon as you ventured out. Anti-freeze? What was that? We had never even heard of it! Many a radiator have I soldered at night for lads to get to work next day.

It was just after the hardest winter in living memory that I was setting up on my own, and at about this time, (1948 to be precise) that I acquired another three acres of land making my little farm 25 acres, and I still had a full-time blacksmith's shop to run!

Catching a pony can take as long as the actual job of work. Horses can be awkward devils when you are in a hurry, which reminds me of an anecdote about a horse dealer who claimed never to have told a lie.

In the pub one night he told one of his mates he had sold such-and-such a horse that day. His mate was quite surprised, as he had been trying to sell that particular horse for quite some time. 'That's lucky,' he remarked, 'Did you tell the buyer you couldna catch the bugger.'

'He never asked,' was the canny reply.

All this is leading up to how I came to buy my first tractor. In 1948, there were not many good second-hand tractors about. They were quite scarce in fact. One problem was WHEN to buy, another more pressing and far bigger in my case was finding the money. A farmer came into the shop one day and I asked him : 'Where can I find a good second-hand tractor?'

'Go and try Jones Brothers in Llangollen.'

Llangollen was in another country and 15 miles away, I suggested. But he was adamant : 'You go and pay him a visit.' Saturday afternoon, I got 'on me bike' to Llangollen to be met by Mr. Jones.

'Can I help you?' he asked.

'Yes, please,' was my courteous reply. 'I want a second-hand tractor.'

'How much do you want to pay?'

'As little as possible.' I said.

'There is an Allis B there — good runner — for £130 — 'anna done a lot of work.'

I nearly jumped on my bike to head back home to Frankton. I hadn't got £30, never mind £130.

'What's your problem?' he said.

I told him I would have a job to find £30 never mind the other £100.

'Tell you what,' he said. 'If you find the £30, you can have it and pay me the other £100 over twelve months — eight pounds, ten shillings a month.'

'Thank you very much.' was my reply.

Arriving home, my mother asked, 'Well, how did you get on?' I explained the position.

I managed to get a bit of money owing to me — remember,

a quarter's credit was given, and expected, in those days in business. My mother found a few pounds, so did my brothers and the major figure of £30 was achieved.

I went back to Llangollen the following Saturday, 'I've got the £30.' I said. (which Mr. Jones did not even bother to count) 'Right' he said 'She's your tractor but remember, £8 10 shillings a month for twelve months.' As I drove the Allis home, I felt like a king. 'My own tractor' — not even thinking how the hell I was going to find the other £100 — impetuous youth I suppose.

The Allis B tractor was possibly the most unsuitable tractor for a banky farm. It was fine with its own fitted implements, such as a mid-mounted mower, and other implements that could be mid-mounted (for row crop work) — but not for connected horse-drawn implements that were all hitched up to a draw bar at the rear-end.

Many precarious journeys with a cart load of muck were achieved. The front end would come up — which meant you had to drive on independent brakes which would lock the back wheel independently to allow you to turn and steer.

Nevertheless, within a few weeks and with the weight of a couple of 56-pound weights bracketed on to the front axle, Allis became a very important piece of machinery. At least you didn't have to go and catch her — but as with all machinery in those days, you had to swing her to start. Strangely enough, Allis would start with no trouble, but if you stalled her when she was warm or turned her over to T.V.O. too soon before she was warm, you might as well leave her in the field or yard until she was stone cold. No amount of swinging or cursing or kicking the back wheels, Allis would only start from cold.

Many wrists of farm lads have been broken through swinging Allis B tractors when warm — which reminds me of the story of a farmer who claimed he had swung Allis for four hours, got her boiling and she still would not start! After keeping Allis for about three years with all her whims and problems, a 'Fergie' was the tractor to go for — a petrol Fergie with a battery start — but at what price?

After months of thoughts and a few sleepless nights, off

18

again to Jones Brothers at Llangollen to see Mr. Jones. Before I had a chance to say anything, he spoke first : 'You've come to change Allis for a Fergie.'

I said 'Yes, but how did you know?' 'Oh, its the general pattern, lad.' he said. 'The Fergie is a very popular tractor — one there, grey, a petrol model, is £180. Allis is worth about £80 so I need about another hundred pounds off you to change.' The same procedure — £100 to be paid over twelve months — no paperwork — a shake of the hand. Another deal struck. Country trust again.

I asked him in later years, 'Why did you trust me?' His reply : 'I knew your dad and he never loosed anyone down, so I knew you wouldn't'.

I kept that little grey petrol Fergie for many years. By this time, second-hand hydraulic implements were starting to appear at farm sales and machinery dealers' yards and with the aid now of electric welder, etc. the Village Blacksmith was able to repair or alter them a bit if needed.

A reason for recalling the story of my first tractor more than forty years ago is a sequel less than two years ago. I have put together quite a collection of tractors; two Allis Bs and Petrol Fergies, quite a collection of old farm machinery and quite a number of visitors call because of my writing these books.

That afternoon, two years ago, two dear ladies came into my yard. I will, with respect, call them 'Senior Citizens'. They were very interested in my collection of farm and blacksmith's machinery and I told them the story of the buying of my first two tractors — the Allis B and the Fergie — and how Mr. Jones of Llangollen had trusted me. Without his help and trust, I said I could not have bought them. There was a tear in one lady's eyes and I enquired whether she was not feeling well. She said I was talking about her father all those years ago. I believe I was not the only one he helped.

There is not much more to add except to say : 'Thank you Mr Jones for all your help.'

Chapter 3

The Machine Takes Over

THE grey Fergie tractor's popularity with the British farmer was certainly instrumental in the demise of working shire horses on farms. Apart from one or two farmers who remained loyal to the shire, Mr. John Suckley, at Brogyntyn, by Oswestry, and later, Brian Davies, Park Hall Farm, Oswestry, they almost disappeared completely.

There were however still a few hunters and ponies to shoe in the area, but the main job of a blacksmith became the repair of implements and the conversion of odd horse-drawn implements to tractor-drawn. Electric welders and drills had by now appeared. Electricity came to Frankton in about 1950 — this may have been the first sign of modern progress. The lad who, when leaving school, started off by blowing the bellows in a smithy, was made redundant.

It was the start of progress or streamlining, not just in the village Smithy but throughout country life. By now most farmers and smallholders had purchased a milking machine. The hand milker, with her stool and bucket, who would milk four or five cows morning and evening by hand, was disappearing.

As we have progressed through the years, one worker with the most up-to-date and sophisticated machines can milk 100 cows an hour, and in some cases as many as 200 cows on his or her own. One farmer, Glyn Baker of Easstwick was heard to remark about his parlour: 'We call it the Snake Pit — you snake into it and you be b . . . . . glad to snake out of it.'

I, too, had by this time branched out to a milking machine — one which would milk about three cows at a time — with a

20

little one-horse motor, a small vacuum pump and three units. Vera was made 'redundant' but did not receive any redundancy money! Instead she had to clean and scrub the teat cups in a big old bath. I think she would have rather milked cows by hand — there's not so much cleaning with a cow milked by hand. Officialdom was now appearing — gone were the tests undertaken by the lorry driver, Alf Whitfield or Frank Davies (and many other drivers, too numerous to mention who had their regular rounds). I know that when you write things down you must get your facts right but I believe at one time there was more milk produced in an eight-mile radius of our little town of Ellesmere than anywhere else in the world.

The new phrase, 'Milk Inspectors' was being spoken, sometimes in whispered terms, and by various not always complimentary names. A smelly teat cup, a blocked drain or getting a churn of milk back, meant you knew that you were 'on the rack' for about a week with extra visits from the Inspectors and extra tests down at the United Dairy. We sometimes held them in awe but I expect they were only doing their job. Later came the S.N.F. tests — not enough butter fat could also get you into trouble and as I have already said many times, it was amazing how many people made a living out of the 'Old Cow' and if you could go through the summer months without having any sour milk back (and only one letter from your Bank Manager), life was going along quite well. By now, I had the marvellous overdraft allowance of £100, reviewed every twelve months and I still have in my possession a letter from the bank, telling me to withold any further drawing as I was £6 overdrawn. The letter arrived the day my daughter died — I was obviously not destined to become a Robert Maxwell.

Chapter 4

Farming Parasites!

AMONG new names that were appearing in farming circles at this time were farm manager and estate agent. I have many friends in farm management but I think it is quite simple to farm with other people's money rather than your own and some estate agents I think of as parasites on farming society.

Selling off old country estates resulted in funds being drained out of the countryside to pay off crippling death duties. Estates and farms were bought by syndicates, insurance companies and the like. Profit at all costs was the cry — never mind raping the land to produce massive buildings, concrete yards and slurry pits (in many cases grant-aided)! Milk more cows, put up rents, farmers running around to keep the faceless ones in towns and cities in funds, rent reviews every three years, get on or get out! were the order of the day.

Was this really farming? In my humble opinion, No. As I have said many times where will it all end?

I am afraid it has ended in Brussels. At last the economic boom has crashed. What price now the whiz-kid farm manager and estate agent growing three tons to the acre when you can get more from the Government by not farming, through Set-Aside — another new word! Still they had a good run. Running their cars, and paying their inflated salaries were an unnecessary expense on farmers' annual cycle, but I suppose 'Live and Let Live!'

I have often wondered what use, if any, they are to the farming community, these people who are not really worth their salt, have read too many books, and have a couple of letters after their names. Farming and blacksmithing are not exact arts, not always carried out according to the Book, no matter how many qualifications you have. If it does not rain at the right time, or if it is too dry, it is no good saying 'The Book Says, Sow by such and such a date, or harvest at such and such a time. If the Good Lord does not send the right weather, dozens of books will not help and a Cirencester Tie is no better than any other. Still I suppose you can always put up the rents of the tenant farmer. Anyway we do not want all farmers to retire at 40 with a fortune as there are not enough golf courses for them ! !

Now never mind their wives as well — and dare I say it now, I think there is going to be a major problem with the advent of women taking up this noble sport which at one time was a man's sole domain. With their new found freedom from the kitchen sink and washday blues, with the arrival of the microwave oven, hubby can now be left to get his own dinner or tea and often has to.

I don't know which can be the most boring when talking about their golf but a tip I can give other golfers is when ringing up to have a word with the husband, if the lady golfer answers, before she has chance to tell you of her latest round, just say quickly 'What did you score on the 17th ?' and hopefully, she will forget about the other sixteen! Later I will tell of my own golfing days — the laughs and the heartache — and also of helping out Roy Williamson's (The Pro) shop at Oswestry. Having been a blacksmith and dealing with women and horses, there is not a lot of difference between women, horses and women golfers — but a lot more about them later.

Chapter 5

Village Schooling Lost

1954

The closure of Frankton Church of England School was, in my opinion, one of the follies of Government policy, as was the closure of so many other village schools. A few of us villagers made a token protest to the authorities but we were not strong enough and accepted the bribe of a free bus to Ellesmere School and also inexpensive dinners for our children as well.

It was my opinion then, and is still my opinion now, that the smaller children up to the age of say, ten, should be brought up as near as possible to their own environment with their mothers at home and able to walk to school and in lots of cases, go home for dinner as well. Mums were at home at dinner time as the advent of working mothers had still to arrive. The closure of village schools, soon be followed by the closure of the village railway stations, were two of the most retrograde steps ever taken. Soon came the closure of the village shops and so therefore, the Death of the Village.

Promises of a free bus and free meals soon went by the board and a small charge was made for these items, soon to be increased. Bit by bit, until today, I believe in some cases, it costs up to £2 a day for dinner and transport. Once charges are made, they are never taken off, but it is quite easy to keep adjusting them 'up' yearly — and now, in our case, the school at Ellesmere, where something like 450 children attend, is under threat of closure. Villages like Welsh Frankton and small towns like Ellesmere should be protected from various Governments' whims and proposals. When young people move away, as many

24

have to, to find work, it is not just the Death of a Village, but also the Death of a Town. I have witnessed the closure of a lot of industry around our little bit of Shropshire; industries that provided a living for its many small town and country dwellers. Gone, I am afraid, for ever . . . where? These industries created enough work for a village or town, when people could walk to work, or take a short journey on a bike. Today, a car is needed to go as far as thirty or forty miles — to be no better off financially. More money, perhaps — but does it go as far?

Village children being brought up having 'mod cons' at school, when they bring new-found friends out into the country cottage, had to tell them that the outside toilet was situated at the bottom of he garden, surrounded by laurels and a privet hedge.

That brings me back to Estate Managers. They put a new toilet in but charged extra rent. Then the spiral started, — extra rent meant extra pay — extra pay meant extra cost on a job — extra cost, extra inflation — and so it went on.

Speaking from experience, one could not find a cow man in the 60s and 70s to help with the milking of a dairy herd. A man could earn more money for a lot less hours in a factory. What was 'Saturday morning' working? Soon 'What was Friday working?' — More time off, more leisure time, more money needed for pleasure — A caravan on the coast, then a boat, then join a golf club — as I did in 1959 when subscriptions were £6 a year! Now, in some cases, hundreds of pounds a year to be a member.

Various Golf Societies were formed and so many names. I am not going to try and mention them. 'The Swinging 60s and 70s' — Less work, more pay. The bosses of Industry and Commerce were no better. They wanted to play golf every afternoon, travelling in their XJ6 Jaguars whilst a strike was taking place at their factories. 'Give 'em more — get them back to work.' was the cry to many Government ministers. This was going on all over the country — whilst the Germans and the Japanese were slowly building and reconstructing their factories, taking over our foreign markets. I saw all this from my Smithy door.

Gone were the days when you could ring up British Oxygen at Crewe for oxygen and acetylene on a Saturday morning and get a delivery on a Monday. Soon a week's notice was required, as was the cheque for it before you had the product — and then if you had no help to load and unload the cylinders, the driver (not in all cases but in many) would drive away. No supplies that week.

I once said to one minor official on the telephone in his office 'If I am not at my Smithy when the driver arrives, ask him to go to the house and my wife, Vera, will give him a lift off and on with the cylinders.' His reply to me, in no uncertain terms was: 'Don't hide behind the skirts of women!' It was not always convenient for a village blacksmith to be in his Smithy at certain times. Gone were the days when a village blacksmith worked in his Smithy all day. Diversification had started. To cope in a Smithy, the blacksmith had to be mobile, with all the problems that started to bring. Gone were the days when a waggoner would bring his implements to be repaired. 'Move with the times.' I was told. 'Get on, or get out.' Another old country rhyme reminds us:

> Life is to be lived.
> Money is to be spent.
> Piddle in the pot —
> Or get off it!

— meaning if you are not going to have a go yourself, let somebody else. Having said that, BIG is not always BEAUTIFUL or the BEST as I believe some of the bigger arable farms are starting to find out. It will never alter the old saying 'When the farmer is doing well, the country is prospering.' as there is no better spender than the farmer.

This chapter started off with the closure of the village schools and ends with the Death of Village Cottages! They were being sold off to 'Townies' and became too dear for the village lads to buy. Little cottages made thousands of pounds! People buying them did not know the Country Code of 'Give and Take'. If a cow, sheep or pig got into their garden, solicitors' letters were soon flying about — but if their dog ran the same animals in the field, that was alright. Very often, an aborted calf, months premature from a heifer or cow that had been chased by a dog was the result. Quite recently, a woman had let loose a couple of Rottweilers in one of my fields where two of my grandsons were playing. They came screaming to the house as she had lost control of her dogs. I went out with a large stick and told her in no uncertain terms what I would do to the dogs with a 12-bore gun if it happened again. The fact she was trespassing on private property did not matter to her — and she informed me I would be hearing from her solicitors. This incident happened a few years ago. I am still waiting for that letter. Is the life of a child less important than the life of a dog? Surely we must start to get our priorities in the right order. By the way, I have been a dog-lover all my life.

Sadly, I finish this chapter off regarding the closure of a village school — it is, in my opinion, the Death Knell of a village. One half of the village does not know the other half. It will never be the same again. Gone for ever, the community spirit where everybody knew everybody and their problems. Gone the bartering system — give and take — make allowances for other people's shortcomings. Yes, my age group has witnessed all these changes and as Alistair Cooke in one of his 'Letters from America' once said, 'It has all happened in our time.'

Chapter 6

Wheels and Axles

THE work of the village blacksmith was changing. Horse-drawn implements had to be converted to tractor-drawn — draw-bars instead of shafts, rubber wheels replacing iron wheels, pre-war lorries being scrapped, axles dismantled — sold to scrap dealers. One particular scrap dealer in a village not far from Welsh Frankton bought a lot of axles and wheels off old cars and lorries and of course, had got them for sale to black-smiths and wheelwrights, etc. On an evening visit with Eric Jones, Ron's dad, to this particular scrap yard, in about 1950, the bloke who owned the scrapyard had a rather large family — possibly a dozen children of all ages seemed to be always there. Toilet facilities in many cases, were behind a scrap lorry. 'Tread carefully.' was the order of the day. This particular night, there were as always, two or three lurcher-type dogs about and one of the kids was eating the largest buttie I think I have ever seen. After taking a bite out of it, he held the buttie so that this darned big crossbred lurcher could take a bite out of it as well. The expression on Eric's face was flabber-gasted and his remark to this lad was, 'You dirty little b . . . . . Why did you let him do that for?' The reply from the lad was, 'He is a pedigree, sir!' I can't add much more to that tale — only that that big family of children all grew into respected citizens. I remember many years later being at a show and they had a horse in an American-style trotting race. I asked the lad leading the horse: 'How much is he worth?'

The reply, without hesitation, was 'Your pocket inna' deep enough!' No punches pulled.

Talking of axles and wheels — a Mr. Percy Culham, who eventually moved into this part of the world from London was, at that time, in the Police Force. He must have had contacts down there because I can remember he used to send up axles and wheels by train to Gobowen for Eric Jones to put on carts and also to sell. At that time, there were not enough axles and wheels to satisfy the demand from farmers.

Farming was on the move in the fifties. Fertilisers were being used in larger quantities to grow more grass — to get more milk — keep more cows to the acre — and the spiral started. First calf heifers were bred to give five gallons a day. Now, I believe with better breeding and using selected bulls, ten gallons a day. Is it old fashioned to talk in 'gallons'? I suppose it should be 'litres'.

My own life was becoming far more hectic. The twelve acres at the Perthy consisted of five smallholdings. Jack Speke farmed about 2.5 as did Dave Phillips. Tommy Jones had passed away and Hilda had moved to Ellesmere — another 2.5 acres Edwin Roberts and Walter Humphrey another five acres. In a year or two all the acreage was eventually put to Perthy Smithy so, with Hardwicke Paddocks as well, I was farming something like forty acres, with a blacksmith business to run as well. The arrival of our second daughter, Valerie, meant Vera could not do as much on the farm. On many occasions, the pram was pushed to the farm yard when help was needed. We also had a full-time man to help run the farm — Sid Jones was his name.

The arrival of our daughter, Valerie was not as straight forward as most births. Valerie had decided she was going to be born feet first — I believe a more difficult birth — and due to the fact that we had lost our first child, Dr. Lloyd decided that Valerie should be born by Caesarean section. This happened at the old R.S.I. on 8th October, 1954 not as is the case today — husbands were not allowed to be there. However, next day, Saturday, come 2 o'clock, away I went, not knowing how I was going to find Vera. With a bunch of grapes and a few flowers, I arrived to find Vera sitting up in bed having just had a big dinner — I had wasted the grapes!

Sid was not used to driving tractors and one day came into

the Smithy and asked me to go with him down to the bottom field to look at a drain. I said, 'Right, I'll come now.'

'You drive the tractor.' he said.

I said, 'No way.'

We got to the field, Sid driving very cautiously, when I shouted to him, 'Stop — for God's sake — Stop!'

He did the opposite. He opened the throttle up and we went round the field at a fair old bat. Eventually, we pulled up not far from the wood hedge. I was laughing by this time and Sid said to me, 'What did you want me to stop for?' I said 'Nothing — I was only testing you!' I thought he was going to hit me but all was well and we had a laugh together. Eventually Sid left. I think he was of retiring age and as I have mentioned earlier, cowmen were hard to come by — so our first milking machine was bought from Fullswoods in Ellesmere. Duncan Jones and Mervyn Morris put it in for me one Saturday — two units and a spare bucket — Automation had come to Perthy, two cows milked at the same time! Today six or eight — I'm not quite sure.

Horses were now starting to appear — or I should say, ponies. The 'in' thing was to buy a son or daughter a pony and, in a later chapter, I will tell of some of the sad incidents that I have come across regarding the neglect of ponies due to the ignorance of a lot of people who have acquired them. A pony has feelings and should not be discarded like a bike your son or daughter has grown tired of. A pony needs a worm drench twice a year, feet cutting at least four times a year, a decent field, and shelter from all the elements (wet, cold winds, sunshine and flies). In fact, a pony needs a lot of care and attention; the more love and affection given them, the more pleasure you will have with them.

Chapter 7

Women With Horses

WOMEN and horses fall into various categories and I am now going to try and identify them — having met with all sorts in the last 55 years! If my memory serves me right, I took the first shoes off a horse for 'Me Dad' at about the age of eleven :

Category 1

In category one, we have the grannie who had her first ride on her dad's old cart horse and who is now possibly 50 to 60 years of age. The old cart horse she first rode would have had a bridle with the blinkers cut off — possibly tied up in places with a bit of binder twine. Some of her fondest memories would be of bringing the old cart horse to be shod at our Smithy which was very similar to any other village Smithy before the war or just after.

My mother could make some smashing lemonade or Mason's extract another kind of pop, and a lump of her home-made currant cake would have been a treat for many farmers' daughters.

Maybe some farms would have a working pony — a Welsh Cob with a bit more speed than the old cart horse. Perhaps a saddle would come with this pony — not a bit of sacking like the old cart horse had. In the Christmas holidays they might be allowed to go to see the local hunt perhaps imagining themselves to be a future Fred Archer.

Today, their time is spent at weekends mainly at Pony Club events with their grandchildren, driving the old Land Rover or a big old estate car and perhaps an old trailer that had seen better days. The Land Rover or estate car will be full of everything that goes with horses — not forgetting flasks of coffee, butties and a few apples.

The 'Grannie' figure can also be seen on the old push bike that's been in the barn for many a year. Yes, you can meet them on these bikes around the country lanes warning any Tom, Dick or Harry in their Ford Escort that the grandchildren are around the next corner and Heaven Help Them if they don't slow down.

I suppose if you asked that 'Grannie' figure which were her happiest days, you would get the reply 'Now', the reason being that she now has more time to spend with her grandchildren than she ever had with her own children. Also, the 'Grannie' type of person is always the first to help with Riding for the Disabled and is also 'in on the act' for the Pony Club etc. Yes, 'Grannie' and her horses have always figured highly in my estimation. They have the ability to get more haughty-types of people to help out at gymkhanas. So I put the 'Grannie' No. 1 on the list of favourite women.

Category 2

We now come to women who never had a pony or horse themselves. In fact — clueless — as are their husbands. But, they have bought their daughter a pony (mainly because the daughter's friend has one) — the 'in' thing to do.

These ladies are to be helped as much as is humanly possible, not for their own sake, but more importantly, for that of the ponies.

They are the type of people who would put an electric fire in the pony's stable and heat hot water bottles to keep the pony warm during the winter months — very gullible to all and sundry.

They don't know whether you are 'pulling their leg' when you tell them that their pony is too fat and that they should cut down his corn and also keep him in and off the fresh grass in the spring of the year. They will look at you in disbelief until you explain how ponies can get fever in the feet if they are allowed to gorge themselves and that Fever in the Feet or Laminites is one of the worst possible complaints a pony can get.

They take no notice and then the inevitable happens — you get a phone call telling you their pony is lame and asking what they should do. Then you tell them to bring the pony in immediately and to only give it a small portion of hay and a bucket of water and no more and to hose down the pony's feet with cold water (or better still, to stand them up to their hocks in running water or a cool pool) and to get the vet to give them pain-killing injections. All this caused through not understanding that you must be cruel to be kind.

In many cases, I have known the mother to be secretly giving the pony currant cake, apples and chocolate because she felt sorry for the pony as 'he always seemed to be hungry'. She was, in fact, doing the pony much more harm — but I suppose it's trade for the Veterinary Surgeon to have to go and treat such ponies.

Category 3

Now this one is the woman who had a pony herself, went to all the shows, gymkhanas, Pony Club meetings, but did not win anything due to her lack of skill and the shortcomings of her pony. She has a daughter and she has bought her a pony. She is determined her daughter is going to do the winning that she was incapable of.

Unfortunately, the daughter is not half as keen as her mother and in fact, is more interested in the opposite sex. Now, this mother, I feel sorry for. She works really hard, probably in most cases at a part-time job, to supplement the family income and the keep of the pony. She is the one who rings up the blacksmith, the one who brings the pony to be shod, or is at home whenever the blacksmith arrives. I really don't know why she bothers but perhaps she is trying to re-live her childhood and revive childhood memories, always willing to ask for advice and to make a welcome cup of coffee for the blacksmith.

Category 4

Now we come to No. 4. This girl had a pony when she was about six years old and has now acquired a larger pony 14-2 and she has been professionally trained to ride and is college-educated, talks a bit 'far back' — altogether a different education to that of the village blacksmith. Education is not everything in this world and I sometimes feel that if common sense and respect for others were on the school curriculum, we could have a better country. However, this is only my opinion. I am only telling the reader about the experiences of a village blacksmith after 55 years of being in the horse world and the old saying is true — 'It takes all sorts . . .'

Category No. 5

Now we come to the woman who, unfortunately, is a little bit short of what matters, in this world today — the ability to to pay her way. She can be seen at the odd horse sale, hoping to pick up a Grand National winner for a few pounds. She invariably runs a clapped-out old big banger which pulls a small clapped-out trailer. She knows that if she buys anything, she would have a job to get the local haulier to transport it for her (unless she produced the 'readies'). However, she keeps going year after year, paying the blacksmith, and everyone else, now and then — always moaning about the price of shoeing, vet's bills, corn, etc.

Category No. 6

Now we come to the Assistant Instructor or Riding Instructor. It means they charge for giving lessons to other people. Invariably, they own a Riding Centre or work for a Riding School. These people, I have always felt, live in a world of their own, possibly because in many cases, they have to work at weekends when other people have time off. If they are the owners, they are not too bad but if they ar only working for a Riding Centre, Saturdays and Sundays are not the best times to 'pull their legs'. Their sense of humour, if they ever have any, is switched off. Should it be a bad day (a row with a boyfriend perhaps heaven help any poor youngster who goes left instead of right or bounces down when she should bounce up, leans back instead of forward. The noise that some I.'s and A.I.'s can make sometimes makes me wonder whether they ought to have joined the army. Sergeant Major crowns on their sleeves would, I think, not be out of place. However, thank God, quite a few I have met are reasonably normal — well, as 'normal' as can be in the circumstances — and in many cases, will take advice from the blacksmith and occasionally will even ask for advice.

Category No. 7

The Horse-dealing Woman — who also deals in any form of riding equipment, i.e. saddles, bridles, horse rugs — knows all the latest cures. In fact, she knows, or thinks she does, more than the vet, the blacksmith, the worm drench rep., the corn merchant, or the horse dealer put together. In fact, she knows more than God. She knows more than anybody and is usually OWING everybody. They come in all shapes and sizes and their hair can be any colour (according to what bottle they use). Some have forward teeth, some a few teeth, and quite a few no teeth at all. She wears black riding boots, highly polished tight-fitting jodhpurs, tweed hacking jacket with the middle button sewn higher on (trying to define a waistline or where the waistline used to be).

She probably has a couple of Hunters and a two year old turned out in some farmer's field. Whether she owns them is very doubtful — or whether she owns anything at all equally so.

She rings up the blacksmith and more or less demands her horse be shod — never mind whether anyone else is booked in.

Appointments are very difficult for her to keep. A horse booked in for 9 o'clock on Monday morning — 8.30 a.m. the phone rings — 'Sorry, car (the clapped out Jaguar) won't start — can you do a favour and pop out and put one shoe on as there's a customer coming in to see the horse which is for sale?' You go to put one shoe on, hoping that she will be able to sell the horse and when you arrive, you very often find that she has three shoes off. That you have another horse booked in at 10 o'clock is irrelevant to her.

Yes, this horsewoman is a Classic. She can curse you one minute, next moment, a flood of tears. A lot of them are strangers to the truth. They will look you in the eye and promise to pay you your bill and a few weeks later, you find they have gone to another blacksmith. I recall one woman in this category once saying to me that she had dealt more in thousands than I had seen hundreds.

Thank God all women and horses are not like this. They are only a small percentage — but just to recap, there is not a lot the matter with horses but I say this without fear or favour. A third of people who own horses should not and if they take offence at what I have written, so be it. That's what it was intended to do.

I am afraid there is not a lot of good that I can say about this type of horsewoman though I suppose life would have been a hell of a lot duller and the rest of this page is recorded what this type of woman knows about a horse and as you see, it is blank!

Chapter 8

'Snowball'

MY daughter, Valerie had her first pony in about 1962. 'Snowball' was her name, with a bit of age — but a perfect first pony. She had belonged to a lad who was deaf and dumb, little did I realise from that day what the problems, tears and heartbreak that were to follow. We had an old Land Rover at that time, borrowed a trailer of Bryan's and away to a Mr. Rutter's farm not far from The Cock, at Barton. £50 was the price of Snowball and a saddle and bridle were included. We arrived back at the Perthy blacksmith shop before Valerie came home from school. Vera had, by this time, tied a little cord on to Snowball's mane, saying, 'My name is Snowball and I now belong to Valerie Strange'.

The look on Valerie's face when she arrived home from school said it all. As I suppose, thousands of other children had expressed the same look over the years on having their own first pony. Snowball settled in quite well and soon became a friend of the family. Yes, and even to the villagers.

There is something about a pony that I find hard to describe. If you treat them with kindness, the rewards you will get are countless. Snowball would go on her own down to the house for a bit of bread or some other titbit Vera would give her and if the house door was open, she would go and help herself to anything that was going spare on the table. At times, if all the doors were open, she would go right through the house and out through the front door and back up the yard.

This brings me naturally to the story of Snowball and the stew. Alan, our son, I suppose would be about seven at the time. A Saturday it was, I shall never forget that day. We always had a saucepan of stew on Saturdays. That was the day that Bill used to come and work for us (affectionately known as 'Tote'). On the Friday before, Vera had just finished papering the kitchen and also the ceiling.

Snowball had come down to the house as usual to find Alan in on his own. He got the saucepan with the left over stew in and proceeded to feed Snowball. Now, as all horse people know, horses very often blow through their nostrils when they are feeding — a sort of Brrrr . . . This, Snowball did many times!

Consequently, the walls, the ceiling, everywhere were covered in left-over stew — bits of carrot hanging on the curtains — a few peas splattered over the walls and windows — and gravy everywhere! Mum came in, Snowball disappeared up the yard, Alan had to be changed and bathed and the rest of us kept out of the way until tea-time — by which time, Vera had cooled down a bit and we could all have a good laugh about it. Never again was any stew left lying about!

About that time, it was brought home to me that Alan was not going to be a blacksmith. He was holding Snowball with a halter one day while I was shoeing her. Valerie had said to him 'Hold my pony while I go and get changed.' You know how elder sisters can be — so bossy at times. My son, Alan, was then eight and the likely fourth generation of village blacksmith in Welsh Frankton! Snowball realised that he was not very interested in what he was doing and decided to pull backward across the yard — and Alan was saying to her 'Sit! Sit!' I will not add more leaving it to the reader's imagination as to what my reaction was. But there was a sequel quite recently.

A class of schoolchildren came to the Smithy to watch a blacksmithing demonstration. I must have been looking a bit faint and weary, because one little fellow asked: 'Alf, when you finish demonstrating, who is going to take over?'

I told him how I realised my son was not going to be a blacksmith, quoting the story of Alan telling Snowball to sit.

Quick as a flash, he commented: 'He would make a good dog handler.'

Chapter 9

Forging Ahead

LIFE was becoming quite hectic. It does not seem much today to be milking 25 cows and being a full-time blacksmith with only the help of Norman as week-end milker and casual labour for seasonal work. Forty acres was the total acreage at that time, but out of the blue came the chance to take over Brow Farm — another 60 acres, involving, I suppose the biggest decision of my life up to then. The total acreage would rise to 100.

By now, I was 40 years old, and a lot of thought was given to this new venture, for it meant bank managers on my back again, advisory officers to be listened to, Bernard Hallett my accountant to draw up plans, budgets to be got out (knowing damn well they would never be met) and many sleepless nights.

Eventually the decision was made to have a go. 'Better chance for your children,' I was told. We moved to Brow Farm in September 1965, a move of 100 yards. I was not aware of it at the time, but quite a unique situation arose when I was taking over the tenancy of Brow Farm. It is probably one of very few occasion that it has happened that the outgoing tenant, in this case Bryan, the ingoing tenant, myself, and the landlord, Col. Kynaston all requested Jim Pearce to act for them. He was a personal friend of Bryan's and the Strange family connection went back a long while, probably through three generations, as he too was of blacksmithing stock.

His fair valuation was agreed by all three of us, and I wonder whether this had ever happened before. For the benefit of non-farming readers it is perhaps necessary to explain that when a tenancy is taken or relinquished, a three-way valuation often becomes necessary where the incoming tenant takes over crops and fixtrues from the outgoing, and the landlord has also to agree to a valuation of their respective rights between himself and the outgoing tenant — the landlord paying for any improvements the tenant has made in recent years or the tenant compensating him for any deterioration that may have occurred during his tenancy.

My overdraft limit, at this time, was £1,000 — no use at all in the new circumstance, so off I went with Bernard to Lloyd's Bank in Ellesmere for our first 'brush' with the new manager, Mr. Jack Stowell. Nine o'clock was the appointed hour. Bernard and I were five minutes early but the bank door was firmly shut. It was suggested by Bernard that we moved up Market Street, a bit away from the bank doors, nearer to Ern. Caseley, the Chemist, so as not to be conspicious.

I felt more like going into the Corner Vaults than the bank. However, we were not outside long before the bank door opened and in we went — Bernard with his immaculate suit, and trilby hat, which he removed as we went through the doors. I don't think I had a hat to take off! 'Mr. Stowell won't be a moment', said one of the girls. Mr. Stowell's door to his office opened and Bernard led the way, undoing the clasp of his briefcase.

I thought to myself, 'Here we go again' — not the Liverpool Anthem but the Alf Strange saga. The office did look a bit brighter than the day of my first visit to see Mr. Brasher, some fifteen years earlier and I suppose, we did now own 25 cows, a few sows, a pony and two children. Bernard had supplied the manager with all the figures for the last three or four years of the Perthy and my overdraft was a bit below my limit. After a while, Mr. Stowell said, 'And how much do you think you will want to borrow?' Lessons had been learned over the previous years. Ask for more than you think you will need — advised Bernard.

'Six thousand pounds.' I replied.

I don't know whether the light in his office flickered or whether his face paled slightly. 'I am afraid, I can't allow that much,' was his reply. 'Well,' I said, 'I have 25 cows and a few pigs, a blacksmith's business, a trade in my fingers.' 'You are short of real capital. Your cows at top value are worth £100 apiece and with your pigs, chickens and so on make £3,000 in total. You would want twice as much from the bank.' 'I am sorry,' I said. 'I have been short of capital all my life and I am not going to Brow Farm without another 30 cows, a better tractor, and I have to put an extension on the present cow house which only ties 25 cows, pipe-lines — all that will take £6,000. I am sorry, but if Lloyd's Bank won't do it, I will have to go elsewhere.' (Where the hell, 'elsewhere' was I hadn't a clue). 'Lloyd's will not come with you but there is a scheme called the Agricultural Credit Corporation. If they take you on, they will guarantee your overdraft at one per cent above bank rate, and it also has to be reduced annually at an agreed figure.' With a nod from Bernard, the forms were signed and a visit was awaited from the A.C.C. A week later, he arrived and as he walked across the yard, I wondered what his reply was going to be. If it was 'no', I realised life was again, going to be a hard grind. As I remember, he was not very old.

'Mr. Alf Strange?' he said.

'It is,' was my reply.

'My name is McGregor and there are a few points I would like to discuss with you regarding your loan.' Down to the house we went for a few forms to sign, a few questions to answer and then his reply was, 'We will take you on.'

With a cup of coffee and a piece of Vera's cake, life seemed to have taken a big turn for the better but we were not 'out of the wood' by a long way. Borrowed money has to be paid for and I also had to start reducing my borrowing after twelve months at the Brow. With the extra thirty cows and another dozen sows, the income on my farming had increased by quite a lot and we were able to afford a full time lad, Ian Mellor. This allowed me to spend more time in blacksmith's shop, which meant more income again. We had our first visit from Mr. McGregor twelve months later, quite happy with our progress, which quite gave me a lift.

41

Chapter 10

Blacksmith at Brow Farm

I WELL remember Mr. McGregor's visit some twelve months later — September, 1967. His first question to me was, 'Mr. Strange, we would like you to buy some land.' I almost fell in a ruck. Me buy land? 'Yes,' he said. 'You are doing more than what you said you would do regarding repayments to the A.C.C. and we feel if you could buy land, we would help you.'

'How much would you lend me?' was my question.

'On your present figures, £15,000.'

At that particular time, £15,000 would have bought about a hundred acres. 'Don't give me your answer. Think about it for a month or two. Give me a ring and we will work some figures out.'

At that time, £15,000 was a hell of a lot of money. I will never know what my decision would have been because a month after to the day, 'Foot and Mouth' broke out in Oswestry Cattle Market (25th October, 1967). That day will never be forgotten in the farming circles of North Shropshire — indeed, it eventually had its effect on the country but it probably affected me more than most.

After Mr. McGregor's visit, my mind went back to the two years before when the decision had been made to come to Brow Farm and taking that big step in one's life. My thoughts turned to the day of Bryan's sale at Brow Farm:

I was standing on my own, viewing the scene — Jim Pearce, the auctioneer, assisted by Ted Bowen doing the selling. It was the last auction for Jim for K. H. Dodd & Bowen as he was moving to a partnership with Hall, Wateridge & Owen. As the auction progressed, I was standing behind two farmers whom I did not know, I overheard one farmer saying to the other: 'They tell me the one that's leaving canna make it go — and the other one that's coming here wunna be here two years.'

I did not make myself known to them because in the farming circles, remarks like that are often commonplace. 'Country gossip' it is called — but it also made me more determined than ever to succeed and prove myself not only to those two farmers, but to many others as well. To progress from village blacksmith to a farmer as well in your own village, you are bound to upset a few. However, I had enough problems of my own without the trivial remarks of others — who could, at times, be very sarcastic and hard. Was it nearly thirty years ago.

Chapter 11

Foot and Mouth

25th OCTOBER, 1967 — Oswestry Cattle Market about noon.

A cow in the market was suspected of having this disease. Over the years, suspect cases had been confirmed or cleared. It is just another occupational hazard the farming community has to live with. Previous cases, over the years, were usually confined to maybe a dozen or so farms.

The usual precautions were taken — suspension of all movements without a permit in a five mile radius of the infection, a brush and bucket of strong disinfectant by the farm gate for all and sundry to wash their wellies or shoes on leaving and arriving at your farm, and in many cases, a barrier of straw placed across the entrance. This was also soaked in disinfectant so that the lorry, car or tractor wheels were also coated with it.

As I remember, we had two outbreaks in the early sixties — in our case, about 1960 and 1961 and all in farming circles thought that this would be similar (closure of markets in a five mile radius) but animals (beef cattle, pigs, etc.) could still be taken to the local abattoir under licence. Milk was still picked up and after the usual ten or so farms had been slaughtered out and no further outbreaks confirmed for a week or so, Restrictions were usually lifted in about a month or so.

Apart from the affected farms, life was allowed to continue more or less as normal — a big 'nuisance' problem more than anything else. In some cases, financial losses did occur in the five mile radius but only for a short time. As our farm, Brow

44

Farm, was outside the restriction area from the farm at Nant-mawr, we were not, for the first few days, put under restriction — which brings me to a little story of the early days of the outbreak. Sam Goff, Secretary of the Oswestry N.F.U. and a big personal golfing friend of mine rang me on the Thursday morning to enquire whether I could take two milking heifers that had been put under restriction in the Oswestry Market and not allowed to be moved back to Glyn Evans' farm at Llansantffraid. As he was quite close to the affected farm, of course I could help him out. He would clear it with the Ministry, obtain the permit and Davey, Sams' brother would bring them with his Land Rover and trailer. That afternoon, after a moment or two of thought and with the assurance of Sam that the risk of my cattle at Brow Farm being affected was virtually nil, the heifers arrived and took their place in my cow house.

Unfortunately, one of the heifers had sustained a badly cut teat and in the farming cicrle term, she 'lost a quarter' but was still milking on the other three quarters. The other one, had she been allowed to have lived, would have made a 'cracking' cow — a good heifer. As fate would have it, we ourselves on 25th November, 1967, contracted the disease and the two heifers belonging to Glyn were slaughtered, as were all of my own livestock.

The irony is that had the heifers been allowed to go home to Glyn's farm, they would have survived because to the best of my knowledge, Glyn's farm did not contract the disease — nor did another of his mates — Glyn Pritchard.

The Monday after Wednesday, 25th, brought home to me that this outbreak of Foot and Mouth was closer than ever. George Brayne, my neighbour went down. One of his cows had contracted the disease, which meant that we were right on the doorstep.

We were very much 'in the thick of it' — Ministry vets practically living on your farm for the following week. But, this time, we escaped. We were very close to being slaughtered out due to the closeness of our farm to George's but after many 'close calls', we were allowed to survive — for the time being.

By now, the disease was becoming rampant. Up to thirty to forty farms a day were affected and we began to realise that this was going to be the biggest catastrophe that Shropshire and Cheshire farmers had ever come up against in recent years. The density of cattle in these two counties was very great and I believe that at that time, the ten mile radius of Ellesmere was the largest milk producing area in the world.

Farmers had now stopped visiting one another and apart from the odd welding job there was no work in the village Smithy. Ellesmere and Oswestry were like ghost towns. News programmes were watched constantly as the carnage went on and on. Farm after farm went down. Telephones were 'red hot' as one farmer phoned another to tell the news of someone else's plight.

Diggers were going up and down our main road in a constant stream as contractors were brought in from areas fifty-odd miles away to dig the graves that all animals had to be buried in — double-quick time. In certain areas, when the ground was not suitable for graves, the animals had to be burned, using tons of coal and railway sleepers.

Some nights, I would wander up to the top of the Brow and see a lot of fires over Cheshire as one farm and another went down. It reminded me of the war time bombing of Chester, Birkenhead and Liverpool — and so the disease kept on. By now, a thousand farms had been affected by the scourge and speaking from my own experience, the pressure was beginning to tell.

I would get up in the middle of the night to look at the cows, fearing the worst, praying that the new next day would be better and not so many farms affected — but it was not to be.

'Had it got out of control?' was the talk. Someone said that he had heard that the Ministry of Agriculture were contemplating a Compulsory Slaughter Policy and that all cattle, pigs and sheep within a certain area were to be put down regardless of whether they had got the disease or not. Drastic measures

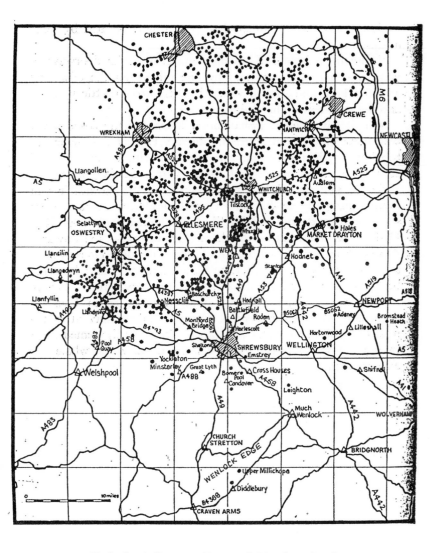

Each dot indicates a Foot and Mouth outbreak.

47

— but I suppose the disease had got to be eradicated by some means or other.

'Hang up a bunch of Spanish onions over the doorways of your cow house.' I was told by one farmer on the telephone and the Foot and Mouth would be attracted to settle in them and not your cows. This, I did.

Whether it worked, I shall never know but the cows in the cow house never contracted the disease. One of our heifers in the bottom field eventually went down with it and, that of course, meant all our other livestock had to be slaughtered.

Before that day, I had that feeling that the inevitable was eventually going to happen. Close neighbours by now were starting to go down — John Elder on Thursday — now, Ron Hodnett on Saturday — the three ridge farms — Joe Edwards (Top House Farm) — Doug. Richardson (Middle House Farm) and John Henry Lewis (Bottom House Farm) — and Joe Clay brothers (one farming Old Cricket, one New Cricket Farms) — but we did not go down until a week or so later — Saturday, 25th November — a month to the day after the first outbreak in Oswestry Smithfield. That month seemed more than a lifetime and even today, I still can relive that whole day in every detail.

Chapter 12

The Day

MY daughter, Valerie, was by now, twelve years old came
with me on that fateful morning to check the heifers in the
bottom fields. Six months later, she was asked to write an
essay on her saddest day and this is what she wrote of. I will
not even try to add anything to that writing, only to let the
reader picture the scene. In a later chapter I will tell of the
reaction and repercussions that morning brought to Brow Farm.

A day or two before that fateful morning, I was starting to
accept the inevitable — only a matter of time. Then, the
Saturday morning arrived — same reaction — milk your cows,
check your pigs and seventeen heifers that were still out in the
bottom fields (although it was late November, there was still
plenty of shelter from the wood).

Valerie and I arrived at the gate and we did not need a
vet to tell us that we had a heifer with Foot and Mouth disease.
She was lying down by the wood — a picture of misery. There
was no need to go right up to her. First priority was to get on
the phone to the Ministry Centre that had been set up in
Ellesmere. Symptoms were asked — 'Frothing at the mouth
and also lame.' The disease attacked the tongue and feet. Our
Ministry vet was soon out and confirmed the disease
immediately. The wheels were set in motion for all our animals
to be slaughtered as soon as possible but first, the valuation
had to be made by Jim Pearce, our auctioneer and agreed by
the Ministry vet.

Jim arrived late morning and started with the valuation of
the heifers in the field — 17 in-calf heifers, 16 fit and well and

49

NOTICE

NO ADMITTANCE

ON ACCOUNT OF

FOOT-AND-MOUTH DISEASE

By Order of the Minister of Agriculture, Fisheries and Food.

Form FM23

The Ministry Notice on the gate outside Brow Farm.

wondering what all the fuss was about. A pen was being made to catch them in a corner of the field. This was being made by some workmen who were 'on call' from a pool of men kept in reserve for such emergencies.

No way were the heifers to be brought across the road to the main farm buildings at the Brow. The seventeen heifers were soon penned in, including the sick animal and in a few moments, they were all valued. Then — one of the first shocks that I was to have that day — the request for my double barrel gun and cartridges. I fetched them from the house, and then it really came home to me. The sick heifer was shot in the pen in the field to prevent the spores from getting airborne.

What I did not know at the time is that as soon as a diseased animal dies, the disease dies quickly too. The vet had shown me the sick heifer's tongue — the skin came off in his hand — also the blisters on its feet. The other sixteen heifers were left to await their fate later in the day — much later, as it turned out.

The twelve sows and their offspring were next to be valued, before the cows and calves in the cow house and here again, the cruelty of man carries no sentiment. One sow, and old favourite — one of four that had been bought three years before from Mr. Morris at Chirk, had just started to farrow and had got two little pigs. 'We will come back just now,' said Jim, 'and value her when she has all her young pigs.'

Up to the cow house — sixty cows, all contented, in the cow house — many lying down chewing the cud — as were the two heifers of Glyn's. Jim asked a question about every cow — how old? — when did she calve? — or when was she due to calve? — had I got any pedigrees amongst them? I had one that I had bought off Phil Arthan, Pentre Morgan two years before which was also the mother of one of the heifers in the field. An adjustment was made in the price of the heifer and also the price of Phil's cow was a bit more.

I remembered at the time when I bought the pedigree cow off Phil two years before his remarking: 'She is in calf to a pedigree bull and the calf when born will be worth as much as you have paid for the cow.'

51

The reason Phil sold me the cow was that she was getting on a bit and was a bit rheumaticy and was slow coming in to be milked which did not bother me at that time — but a nuisance in a larger herd.

Back to the valuation — next the calves. I suppose this had taken about an hour from the time of looking at my old favourite sow who then had two pigs. Back went Jim and I and as we looked over the pig sty door, there were twelve healthy little pigs all sucking away at their mother's teats — ten more pigs than an hour ago. A sow and twelve pigs were at that time worth £30 more than a sow and two pigs. The valuation was agreed by the Ministry vet, Jim and me — what next?

By the time the digger had arrived and was digging the grave at the back of the buildings, the cows were looking through the windows of the cow house. Oh, something I forgot was that as soon as we had realised and the vet had confirmed it, a human factor came into play. The vet enquired, before he set the wheels in motion, 'What children have you got?'

'Two,' was the reply, 'Valerie and Alan.'

'What age?' he enquired.

'Twelve and seven.'

'Well,' he said, 'Officially, they are not supposed to leave the farm but if you can get them away, I know nothing.' he said. This was quickly arranged by Vera and Frank from across the road took them with Trixie the dog (who had gone to Mrs. Jarvis's).

Away they all went to Gran's at Welshampton but before she got into the car, Valerie came down to the cow house with tears streaming down her face. She was old enough to realise what was happening. She walked the length of the cow house, looked at all the calves.

The vet was watching her when she suddenly turned round and asked him a question — Would he save one of the calves which she had named 'Legs Eleven' and put it in the cellar where no one would find it? After a pause, the vet turned away. I am sure that he had got a lump in his throat and he did not answer her request. He could not because Ministry policy is to slaughter EVERY cloven hoofed animal.

Valerie and Alan went to Gran's. Jim Pearce, his assistant, and the vet came down for a drink and a butty. I suppose the time would be about two o'clock by now — when the phone went. It was for the vet. He had to leave our farm, go and have a scrub up (car as well) and go elsewhere to do the same procedure. He said 'I will be back to help with slaughtering later in the day.'

By this time, the digger had broken down, having only done about half the grave. The driver was on the phone to get a fitter out as soon as possible but all the fitters from his firm were out 'on call' and then I found out that he, the driver, was not a digger driver at all but worked in the office for the firm'. Apparently, he had been 'roped in'. However, he decided to leave and said he would do his best to get a replacement digger for early next morning — which he did, arriving the morning of Sunday, 26th quite early with the digger on a transporter.

We were not up when he arrived. Now, when he had gone on the Saturday, all the cows were alive and well but when he opened the sliding door and switched the light on, the sight that met his eyes was one he will never forget — sixty cows all dead on their chains, fourteen calves all dead in the bing — a sight he had not bargained for. He knew that the animals were to be slaughtered but the shock was still too great for him. After he had finished digging the grave, he asked his firm not to send him out again on such work.

Ian on the Saturday at about four o'clock, fed all the cows and pigs and milked what cows were milking, only to tip the milk away — no more milk waggons to call for the next six months or so. By this time on the Saturday, the policeman had arrived on the gate. No one was allowed to come or leave, only Ministry officials. Vera, Ian and I did not know what to do.

The waiting was terrible and then the vet's arrival to say that the slaughtermen would be there at about eight o'clock as that Saturday was one of the worst number of outbreaks ever. Then the telephone rang and it was Gordon Lawrence, Sand Hole Farm, New Marton. The slaughterers had just finished there and would be with us in about twenty minutes or so. I went to the cow house to take the message to the vet.

The cows were all still looking very docile but one sensed that they knew lights on at night with men about was strange. I walked the length of the cow house and back. Memories came flooding back to me of my battles to build a herd of cows; the battle with the bank, Milk Board officials — all wiped out in the next two hours or so.

I felt quite sick to think that we had to start all over again. The compensation cheque would obviously go a long way to restocking but the thought of having to do it all again! To literally have to start again — the problems and the heartache that would come with restocking, I will tell later. The vet woke me from my thoughts and said,

'If you don't want to help, Alf, you needn't.'

— a remark I shall never forget as although I had only had some of the cows a few years, a lot of them had come with me from the old home at the Perthy and in many cases, offspring of the cows I had bought from my mother when she moved to her old home at Tetchill in 1960.

As the three slaughtermen arrived, I left the vet and Ian came heavy eyed down to the house at about eight o'clock. I sat by the fire and poured myself a large Scotch. Vera had cut a pile of butties as only a wife can do.

After another Scotch, I felt a bit better, only to have to go into the kitchen. The vet wanted to borrow my two-two rifle as one of the slaughtermen could not get into the one pig sty as the sow with the twelve little pigs was really going mad and an ordinary humane killer gun was of no use in that sort of situation. Sows can be most protective of their young if anyone is going to hurt them — but all to no avail — a rifle bullet into the brain — and they were able to continue their morbid task.

After about two hours, the carnage was over and the vet, Ian and the three men came in for a good wash and clean up. Bottles of beer turned up on the ktichen table, cheese and ham butties, onions and a drop of Scotch for the vet.

As we talked about things in general, one of the lads said it

54

was one of the worst days of his life. He went on to say that he was a professional butcher (as were his mates). He went on to say that he had pride in his work in a Birmingham slaughterhouse. Killing and dressing a bullock was his job.

He said: 'You take pride in your work to prepare the animal for human consumption, but today,' he said, 'I have killed 1,100 animals, left them lying where they fell, little pigs a few hours old lying dead by their mothers. I don't know', he said, 'how you can be so kind as to give us bottles of beer and lovely sandiwches after we have killed all your animals.' At this, the vet said, 'Farmers and country people are brought up with life and death.' and he asked the question, What are you doing tomorrow?' 'I am going home, going to bed and not getting up until Monday morning. I am sick of all the animals I am killing. It is so unnatural. It is like cold blooded murder.'

They left at about 12 o'clock and wished us all the best. We have not heard of them from that day to this.

Chapter 13

The Day After

NEXT day, being Sunday, made no difference, was the start of burying and in our case, 178 animals to be buried in two graves — 17 heifers in the bottom field and 161 at the Brow Farm. Another digger had already arrived to replace the one that was broken and the grave was soon ready. Now started the task of burying all the animals which were dragged out unceremoniously with a chain around their legs or neck. I think the worst part of the operation was that all the animals had to have their bellies slit open to stop them swelling up after they were buried. I believe this had happened on some farms. Just before they were pushed into the grave, their bellies were slit open to reveal calves at various stages — some in the first stages of development — some a few days from being born — pigs, the same.

The job went on, with the grave slowly filling. I remember that the last animal to go in was the boar, alas, not to see a lot of his offspring being born. I have never reckoned up but I suppose really there would be three times the number of animals that had been killed and as I looked for the last time at them, I thought how small they all looked in the bottom of a big hole. Ian's dog, who had been our cow dog, was there and little did we think that in less than a few weeks, he would be buried in the same spot — tragically killed on the Brow — another sad day.

After all the animals had been buried, now started the mammoth job of cleaning out every building, every day for about three weeks — scrubbing with hot water and disinfectant every item, hosing down with cold water — then, do the same tomorrow. A Miss Hall from Ayrshire, a Ministry official, was put in charge.

She used to visit every day and for the first few days, we seemed to have a mixture of workers. A large percentage of them did not want to work. I suppose their pay was not much more than they were drawing on the dole and to have to muck out buildings went very much 'against the grain.' I recall one day, Miss Hall came into the yard and blazed into a couple of these lads because they were having a smoke. I was on the yard at that time and thought she was rather hasty but kept quiet.

One of them had been working a power washer and Miss Hall had told him to get it started and do all the cow houses again. The power washer was engine-driven and after a couple of minutes or so, the lad appeared with a plug in his hand, with a fair big lump of casting attached. Obviously, it had had a fair old smack with a hammer — one could see the piston! A new engine would be required but from where? It would have taken at least a week to find another. I suppose it was one way of dissenting against authority (especially in the form of a woman). I never saw that lad again. Perhaps he went back on the dole. On reflection, he was wrong to break the pump — but ever since, I have tried to see the other man's point of view and encourage rather than condemn.

By now, after the first few days of cleaning, we seemed to have the same three or four men — names I am afraid I have forgotten except for one, Ken Drury from Criftins. Another was a cow man from Evans of Ebnal — farm that had gone down before us.

It was not all 'gloom and doom' though. I recall one of the biggest fellows I have ever seen came into the yard about dinner time to replace the broken down digger. He spoke in a real Irish accent.

It was a time when there was always somebody coming or going — kettle on the boil — butties to be cut — piece of cake — or even a sit-down dinner if there was time. A real community spirit was generated somehow out of that adversity.

'I am going down for my dinner,' I said to this big Irish man. 'Will you come down and have some?'

'No thanks,' was his reply. 'I'll just have a cup of coffee. The doctor has put me on a diet.' (Not before time, I thought, he must have been twenty-stone or more.)

'Do you drink much?' I said.

'That's the trouble,' was the reply. 'I used to drink sixteen pints of draft Guinness every night and he (meaning the doctor) cut me down to ten!'

It was like a little ray of sunshine at a very sad time.

Chapter 14

Cleaning Up and Scrubbing Down

JUST before we went down, everybody was under pressure, including the vets, working very long hours. One night at about eight o'clock, having just finished for the day, there was a knock on the door — vet's inspection. Up the yard we went. The vet seemed a bit agitated and spoke very sharply as he looked the cows over.

'Have any of your cows been off their food, or lame?' He was so very abrupt.

'When was your last official vet's inspection?' For the life of me, I could not remember.

'Come on,' he said, 'you must remember.'

'I'm sorry,' I said, 'but what with one call after another, and the problems of looking after the animals, making sure the corn waggon arrives and is unloaded on the roadside as well as provisions for the house, I canna remember everything.' I could have fallen out with him really and then I had a thought, and asked him, 'Can you remember when you last had a socket?' He paused and then' 'And what do you know about sockets?' 'Oh,' I said, 'I play a bit of golf.' Luckily, so did he, and the mood was broken. Here were two men, both under great pressure, talking in a cow house about their handicaps. Funnily enough, we both played off a handicap of four at the time.

Over a drink down at the house, we shook hands, vowing to have a game when this lot was over — but we never got around to it. Where he came from, I don't know. For the benefit of non-golfers, a 'socket' or a 'shank' is when the ball goes sideways off the club instead of straight — very often called the 'unmentionable' — a soul destroying shot of which I have had many.

After about a fortnight of scrubbing, hosing down and disinfecting, the farm was starting to take on a much cleaner look and we were now organised. Miss Hall was still calling daily — sometimes in the morning — sometimes afternoon. To find out if she had been to John Elder or Ron Hodnett's I would say, 'How are John and Ron getting on?' and she would very often say, 'Oh, I am going there now,' which meant that I gave them a quick ring to say 'She's on her way!' If she went there first, they would ask her. 'How is Alf going on?' and if she replied 'Oh, I'm on my way there now,' — a quick ring to warn me. She once told me that Ron Hodnett, John Elder and I were her best farmers as we were always working when she came!

After about three weeks, our farm was so spick and span — surely the cleanest it had ever been before or since. Some farmers in the area who had not contracted the disease were over stocked due to the closure of all the markets in Shropshire and its borders, and in some cases, were getting short of hay. We farmers who had no cattle, had plenty of fodder. Rob Williams, a mate of mine, had two loads of hay from Brow Farm under Ministry permit for it to be moved to his farm about five miles away.

'Perfectly safe', said the Ministry officials.

'No chance of the disease in the hay barn.'

They were to be proved wrong for Ron discovered in March, 1968 (about five months after he had gone down the first time) that feeding his sheep with hay from his barn, he contracted the disease again. Science and technology are not always right.

Coming to the end of our three weeks of scrubbing, hosing down and disinfecting again and yet again — we were sick of the sight of scrubbing brushes, and the smell of disinfectant everywhere.

A couple of the lads had made a nice little place in the Meal House — a few bags of beet pulp, a few bales of straw. I suppose one could call it a 'den' — for a game of cards. A space had been left to see the road, and the arrival of Miss Hall because our contact with John and Ron had gone (they had finished the previous week, having gone down a week before us). Finally, the ALL CLEAR for Brow Farm came and we were able to go out for the first time in months.

I checked with Ministry officials whether I could go and have a game of golf. 'Yes, but do not visit any farms.'

There was still no livestock in our two mile radius. I can only recall four farms that had not gone down. I suppose, fifty that had contracted the disease. It was coming up to Christmas. What sort of Christmas? How could we celebrate Christmas at such a sad time for all farmers? — not only those who had gone down but also those farmers still living with the dread of being the next to have the disease.

One thing I remember is it would be the first Christmas morning for about thirty years I could have a lie in — no cows to milk — no calves or pigs to feed — only VERY clean and empty buildings to look at.

But the disease went on and on relentlessly — well into the New Year. The compensation cheques were, by now not looking so rosy — no milk cheques — no pigs or calves to sell. Still rents to find, grocery bills to be paid, telephone and electricity bills, cars to be run — and in my case very little work coming into the Smithy.

Towards the end of March there seemed to be fresh hope. No new cases for a couple of days. Was the disease abating or had it finally run its course? Then, Ian, my workman who had been helping at the golf course came home to the Brow and said that one farmer had been allowed to have a few cattle to re-stock one of the first farms that had gone down. If he kept clear for a week or so, more farms would be allowed slowly to have cattle, pigs and sheep again. There was a glimmer of light at the end of a very dark tunnel.

The giving and accepting of credit started to disappear in farming circles. Many farmers were still using corn merchants' credit, but a fairly hefty credit charge was now being put on corn bills (if you fell behind, as many did). Just after the Foot and Mouth epidemic, the general rule was that once you'd lost your credit, well, you might as well use them for the rest of the winter — no point in using bank overdrafts as well. It was brought home to me how cruel life can be in a certain corn merchant's accountant's action to me.

We had, since going down with Foot and Mouth, no income for many months. I had dealt with this particular corn merchant for many years but one afternoon, two months after our outbreak, I received a phone call from their Head Office and the voice on the other end of the phone was quite agitated and very demanding. I was just out of credit time with his firm. He said to me, 'When are you going to square up our account?' I said, 'I will if you allow me to knock off the credit charge that you have put on.'

Who do you think you are? Lord Mayor of London.

'No', I said. 'I am Alf Strange, the village blacksmith from Welsh Frankton.'

'Don't get b . . . . "sarky" with me!' was his reply.

'We want our money and I will see that you pay it fairly soon' — and then words that really hurt me. He said 'You have had your compensation for your cattle.'

'Yes,' I said, 'I have, and for that remark you will now wait for your money.'

Memories of all that we had gone through came flooding back — the loss of all our livestock and seeing them all dead in a mass grave. Here was a jumped-up tuppence ha'ppny accountant telling me what he was going to do. I don't know how much it cost his firm in solicitors' letters but I always used to pay a bit off the account, at the last minute, leaving them to go through the whole procedure again. It would have been twelve months before it was all squared up — an account that could have been settled a little bit more understandingly. Delaying payments was not the way I had been brought up but times were dramatically changing in country life and not for the better. Going fast were the trust and loyalty to all mankind. By this time, the 'Rat Race' had started, even in our village and I believe I am right in saying that this Corn Merchant was eventually, taken over by a bigger concern. Dog eats dog!

Chapter 15

Valerie's Letter

IN March 1968, Valerie, who was at school in Ellesmere was asked to write an essay about her Foot and Mouth experiences. It was to win a prize in a national competition. Because I think it gives a glimpse of how it affected a child. I include what she wrote then :

MY SADDEST DAY

It was a cold, misty morning on the 25th November, 1967. There was quite a thick fog covering all the earth and fields, giving everywhere a very gloomy atmosphere. It was about 8.30 a.m. in the morning and myself and Dad were going down the fields to check the heifers to see if any of them had got foot and mouth.

We left Mum cooking the breakfast, bacon and eggs. We counted the heifers and we only counted 16, there should have been 17. We counted them again and again, but only got 16. We searched the field and eventually, found her lying down by the wood. I knew almost at once she had foot and mouth. I felt just like sinking into the ground and never coming up again. Me Dad sent me on up to the house to get my breakfast and to start feeding the pigs.

I fed the pigs realising it would probably be for the last time. Me Dad came up and I heard him saying to Mum, 'Well, it looks like we have got it.' He rang the centre at Ellesmere for them to confirm it. It wasn't long before the vets were out at the farm looking at the cows but they could not destroy them straight away, this had to be confirmed in London whether or not the animals at the house had to be killed as well. As we thought, they had to be — I hope the man who said this rots in hell !

Later that day the slaughterers came and shot the poor helpless animals. They had no escape from the chains around their necks, it was just like a cold blooded massacre, only worse. It was a matter of a few hours. How anyone can be so ruthless and cruel I do not know. Afterwards they had to bury them. They shot the heifers in the field, then dragged them into a hole. It was just like rubbish going into a bin. Then they covered up the hole. Me Dad said, 'Into that hole went a lot of money and sweat.' My eyes ached for days after through crying. The graves will never vanish and every time I look at them tears creep into my eyes and I hope and pray to God that we never have foot and mouth again.

Valerie Strange
(aged 12)

EPILOGUE

W. J. E. Pearce (May 1993)

I have been asked by Alf Strange to write a short epilogue to his scrap book on the Foot and Mouth epidemic and produce an up to date valuation of the stock which I valued on 25th November 1967 prior to slaughter. Although I have now retired I retain a keen interest in the livestock markets and feel qualified to carry out this request.

The original valuation, as you will see, comprised three separate sheets. Below I give my current valuation figures with the original figures for comparison.

Sheet No.	Description	Valuation 25 Nov. 67	Valuation 8 May 93
1.	30 Dairy cows	£4,420	£26,720
2.	27 Dairy cows	£5,045	£34,445
	7 young cattle		
3.	11 in calf heifers	£2,876 = 10 = 0	£21,772
	6 Friesian bullocks		
	69 Breeding and store pigs		
	Total	£12,341 = 10 = 0	£82,937

In arriving at my present day valuation, it is of interest to note the varying degree in percentage increases of the value of the various classes of stock. The dairy animal for instance has increased it's value by 600-700% or more, whilst pigs have only increased by 300-400%

All through the ages there has always been 'characters', mostly found in country areas and Alf can certainly claim this distinction. Originally the village blacksmith at The Perthy carrying on the family tradition, he then turned farmer until illness forced him to give up both of these occupations. With characteristic enthusiasm he took up writing and to date has already published two successful and popular books; with a third in the pipeline.

This unique record of the foot and mouth epidemic is yet another example of his will to record the daily happenings of the countryside for future generations. Although a grim and tragic story in which I was very much involved as an official valuer, it is a warning of what can happen again should we ever relax the slaughter policy.

To conclude I would like to wish Alf and his wife Vera many years of good health and happiness in their various pastimes and work for charity at The Brow.

W. J. E. Pearce

Chapter 16

A Night Out!

WELSHPOOL market opened for the first time on March 18, 1968, and I suppose that date marks the official start of the end of restrictions on the movement of cattle after a long and dreary five months. That winter had seen the slaughter of 27,000 animals and the payment of £30 million of compensation to farmers as well as a few hundred thousand pounds to contractors for digging graves and for coal and sleepers. It was to be another three months before Oswestry Smithfield opened, eight months almost to the day after the first outbreak. June 26 was the memorable day when both the town and its surrounding areas came back to life. It marked the end of possibly the worst eight months ever in the annals of Shropshire farming. Could it have been avoided if different measures had been taken? We will never know. Was it an Act of God?

After we had gone down in the November, none of us had been any distance away from home, except Valerie and Alan to attend school at Ellesmere.

At the end of January 1968, with Ministry permission, Vera, myself, Valerie and Alan visited my brother Frank at Colwyn Bay. It is a Sunday I shall never forget!

We arrived there in the afternoon after a lovely walk along the beach in a fairly strong wind. After tea at Frank's the wind had reached gale force, and we decided on an early departure for Brow Farm. When we went out to our car, we found a flat tyre and after changing the wheel headed for Shropshire. What a journey! By about seven o'clock, the wind was rocking

66

the car, and we decided not to risk the Horseshoe Pass because of its strength, preferring to travel through Mold and Wrexham.

After leaving Mold we came to a diversion, where a large oak tree had blown down across the main road. We drove on unfamiliar roads, eventually arriving at Summerhill a few miles from Wrexham, the first car to arrive there. There we discovered another large tree blocking our way. Travelling back towards Summerhill, we found ourselves hemmed in by yet another tree that had been blown down after we had passed it.

There was little bit of panic now — two trees were down within less than a half a mile. But there was an outlet — a narrow lane towards another main road. I went there when bang! went the other back tyre when I ran over a large branch with a jagged edge. We could not stop there as we were blocking the lane, so I drove on to arrive on the main road. I opened a field gate, drove my car into the middle of the field, as trees were crashing down all around us, then took stock of the situation. Bedding down Valerie and Alan on the back seat, with our little Terrier dog, Trixie in the middle of them, I decided then to go to the phone box in Wrexham — a distance of about a mile. The gale was really rampant and trees could still be heard crashing down everywhere. I arrived at the phone box, wrenched the door open, when suddenly the wind got into the door and it blew off against the wall — so fierce was the wind. The phone was not working and as I trudged back towards the car, two more trees had come down so I had to walk up the inside of the field (much safer, away from the trees on the road). By now, I suppose it would be eleven o'clock — nothing for it but to spend the night in the middle of a field. By giving the engine a run every hour or so, and with the heater on, it was not too cold but everywhere, as one light after another was switched off, as people lucky enough to be in their own homes went to their warm beds. One had time to reflect on what happend in the past few months and the uncertain times ahead. Would one be able to literally 'start afresh?' Would one have the 'guts' and the motivation to make a go of farming again?

An incident I recall of that night was when a fox appeared

at about 3 a.m. crossing the field in front of the car. Though I switched on the light, he took no notice and went on his way. I must have fallen asleep for I was woken by a policeman, PC Cliff Parry, gently tapping on the windscreen. I wound the window down to hear him ask whether we were all right and what we were doing. I explained what had happened and in less than no time at all we were loaded up into the police car and transported in double-quick time to Wrexham Police Station, where we were given a very welcome drink.

Only after arriving home, by taxi, about 10 a.m. the following morning, did we realise that all we had to eat was a bit of fruit cake we had brought home for my brother Jack's butty box. Fruit cake at three o'clock in the morning in a field outside Wrexham may not appeal as the best of treats, but for us that morning was as good as a banquet! Our Good Samaritan, PC Cliff Parry was, we found out, the father of twin daughters, Janet and Christine, and another daughter, Wendy. His wife was named Edna.

He replaced my tyres at Summerhill Garage and scrapyard, owned by Arthur Jones whose helper was Dave. I believe I am right that 27 years ago they could supply any make of silencer or tyre for cars — the Kwik-fit of yesteryear.

PC Parry also delivered our car back that night. His wife Edna drove his car and as I recall he would not accept any payment, but he did allow me to put two gallons of petrol in his car for his trouble and now some 27 years later I have found out, plays golf on the same course as my brother Frank.

He also that week had 2 letters written about him to the Chief Constable. One was ours praising him for his help on that night. And the other one was written by a woman motorist complaining about him because he had booked her for some motoring offence.

That same night, PC Parry, had been to get some clothes for children who lived in a house whose roof had been severely damaged on the top road at Summerhill. The house had been so damaged that they had to be moved to safer accommodation. As he went upstairs to collect the clothes, the man in the kitchen was far more concerned with rescuing his collection of encyclopaedias.

At another house, where he warned the couple living there that their chimney was not safe and could crash through their roof at any time, he was 'cursed' for waking them in the middle of the night! That night power cables were down everywhere and shop windows in Wrexham were blown in, so severe was the storm. He was on his way home with Sgt. Owen Thomas when they spotted us in the field. PC Cliff Parry later rose to the rank of Inspector, and now lives in retirement at Abergele.

Chapter 17

We Restock

TOWARDS the end of April 1968, we started restocking but I had been allowed to do some blacksmithing, shoeing the odd few horses previously.

Another temporary job I had at that time was as a gamekeeper. Brow Farm is surrounded by a fair few woods — Brow Wood, Salters Wood, Sherwoods Rough and the Cunumbers Wood. They belonged to Col. J. R. Kynaston, who had one of the few surviving herds in our area at that time.

As he had not gone down with Foot and Mouth, George Pryke, at that time 75 years of age, having been gamekeeper on the Hardwicke Estate since 1923 (44 years) could not carry out his duties.

Incidentally George is still going strong and still attending his pheasants — more about him later.

Obviously George was not allowed to come across our land to the wood because of the quarantine regulations. The colonel rang me to ask whether I could see to the feeding of his birds and as I had nothing much to do, it was a nice little job every morning for an hour or so. I say here and now that had I not been a blacksmith, I would have liked to be a gamekeeper — it is so very close to nature.

In the wood one sees the odd fox making its way, warily, always following the contours of the land. Very soon a pheasant would come out of the laurels to feed, they too keeping a wary eye on you. There were not many rabbits at that time due to the myxamotosis epidemic of the 1950s but the odd hare and badger and an occasional hawk hovering overhead added interest to those mornings.

To see the first snowdrop peeping though is another rare pleasure. Something different is to be seen every day of the year in a wooded area.

By the end of March, unfortunately, George was out of of quarantine, and we met one morning in the Cunumbers Wood. I had finally been made redundant after about four months of feeding the birds. My four months as a gamekeeper without a gun is an experience I will remember all my life.

As George thanked me for himself and on behalf of the colonel, my mind flitted back to the 30s, when I was a lad with a catapult, he had chased the village lads and myself around the same woods. How times had changed. But do you know, I never did receive any redundancy pay!

We had also ploughed about 40 acres of our hundred, under a Ministry compensation scheme, so a little bit of money was starting to come in, but we were a long way short of paying our way. I was loathe to go back into the full-time milking of 60 cows again but Ian the cowman had come back to work at Brow Farm and with wages starting to increase and other expenses to be met, the only way was to milk sixty-odd cows again if we were to employ full-time labour. So, the decision was taken to fully re-stock, plus more pigs and a couple of hundred free range hens to sell eggs at the door.

The phone rang one night. Pip Speke, an old mate, a corn merchant, on the other end. 'Do you want to buy some good commercial cows direct from a farm?'

'Yes,' was my reply. 'I could do with another twenty or so. Where are they?'

'Cumberland,' was his reply.

'Cumberland?' I said. 'That's nearly in Scotland!' (He said it was 200 odd miles away).

'How do you know about them?' I asked.

'Bob Griffiths? Area Manager for Criddel's knows some genuine farmers who will sell some of their cows to any farmer who wants some. I'll take you. We'll go up one day, stop the night, see cattle at various farms and come back the next.'

71

Ron Hodnett decided to come as well and away we went. Of course, we took our golf clubs and had a game at Penrith the night of our arrival. Early next morning we visited three farms close by — Joe Ivison (Plumpton Foot), Ramsey Dalgleish (Bulls Head, Plumpton) and George Whitfield (Lowther Gill). We had hired a lorry from Alderton & Huddert Ltd., Great Ashley, Applesy and the lorry driver's name was Jim Hall from that area. He could take eighteen cows on one load so it meant we needed to buy eighteen cows if we could.

What a grand bunch we saw! — eleven in-calf cows from George Whitfield, four in-calf cows from Ramsey Dalgleish and three in-calf cows from Joe Ivison. The deals were struck and the cheques paid in about two hours, then we headed home for Shropshire — with rather less healthy bank balances. This was on Tuesday and the cows were to be delivered on Friday. Something went wrong at the other end and it was another week before the cows were delivered.

One of the cows (a third-calver) was very close to calving the day we bought them. I had my doubts about buying her but she was such a grand-looking cow — the best of the bunch and by far, the most expensive cow that I had ever owned to to that time. I got on the phone to the lorry driver the night before he was delivering the cattle. I said to him, 'Do you think that this cow was too close to calving to travel 200 odd miles?' He assured me he would take all precautions so I felt quite happy about it.

The next day, the cattle arrived and I put them in the bottom field. The cow that was close to calving had travelled well but one of the others had been down and hurt her front leg very badly — apart from her, what a grand lot of cows they looked.

Unfortunately, the cow that had hurt her leg had to be put down — very sad — but we did get a bit of insurance and carcass value at the abattoir so not a serious loss. However, the best cow calved in a couple of days, brought a lovely heifer calf. After she had calved, she took ill and would not eat any corn. George Wyse, the vet called but could not find anything wrong. We tried all forms of remedy — apples, a bit of cabbage leaves but no, she would not eat. George was baffled. After about ten

72

days and dozens of different injections and drenches, she just died. George Wyse went to see her opened at Hordley abattoir but nothing else showed up. He said if he had had to fill in a death certificate, the verdict would have been that she had died 'of a broken heart'.

She had, we presume, probably been too close to calving and had picked her spot to calve in the field she came out of at Bulls Head. Loaded in a wagon, brought 200 miles, she never got over the shock. It was just another hazard of farming that we had to face and accept at the time.

As I have said, farming is not a 'by the book' science when dealing with livestock, but it was, for all that, a very good two days' work.

I finished up with sixteen as good cows as I could wish for — the nucleus of a good herd to build from again. Sadly, I have never met any of those men again. Many times, I have tried to go back to see them, but something has always cropped up. Perhaps this year, I will go. I have often thought about Pip and over the years have often talked about the Cumberland farmers wondering how they too, have fared in the varying economic climate over the years. Is it really twenty five years ago since that expedition?

The digger, the vets, the dead cattle are all so very vivid in my mind, still I have only to close my eyes and the whole scene seems to come to life again — one part of life I would not wish to go through again. Indeed, I would not wish anyone to have to go through such an experience and in that statement, I include farmers who did not contract the disease. They suffered too; not only in mind, but financially, as well.

But now I am going to 'vex or please' many public house debates on the whys and wherefores of who was better off financially — those who had the disease or those farmers who had not.

Yes, it is true that good, fair compensation was paid for the slaughtered cattle, pigs and sheep, but let us not forget, there were no milk cheques for many months, no lambs or pigs to sell. We all suffered, and speaking personally I would say I was no better off for receiving my compensation cheque, and

73

probably quite a lot worse off, for as I have said earlier, the compensation was not over-generous.

When we started to re-stock, my cheque did not buy me what I had lost in the outbreak. I wish I had been kept free of the disease and I write later of the problems I and other farmers had with re-stocked animals.

It is impossible to put a price on some of the problems, not just in financial terms but in human terms. There were instances of close friends, even members of the same family, falling out because one had had Foot and Mouth and several months' enforced idleness, while the other had not, and was envious of the so-called big cheque. One farmer I knew, faced with such a situation, was unlucky enough to be infected a second time. Before the new quarantine had been put into effect, he made an offer to his envious neighbour. 'If you want it, all you have to do is to come to my farm now!' he said. Needless to say, the offer was not taken up!

One of the bigger problems was that the new cows, once they had been turned out into the fields, did not know the position of the gate leading back into the cowhouses. Many had never been chained by their necks in cowhouses, having been used to loose housing and milking in parlours, a completely different technique to the cowhouse milking we were still using. Only later did we install a pipeline and milking units.

An amusing incident was losing one of our freshly bought cows. She did not come in for morning milking, and we only found her later in the day as she had strayed to Reeves, the Buildings Farm. Bill had milked her thinking she was one of his, for he too had all fresh cows. Another big problem was the death of many calves, born quite healthy in most cases, then they would go off their food and fade away after about a month.

After many tests, the conclusion was reached by the vets that they had not had time to build up resistance to certain disesaes that were on our particular farm. I am led to believe that each farm has its different disease problems which cows build up resistance to after a period of time, passing it on to their off-spring. This also happened to pigs and sheep at that time.

There was a scheme to help Foot and Mouth farmers. Canada had donated a very special bull and its semen was to be distributed free to farmers in the area — each allowed a limited number of free inseminations.

I think in our case, about ten free inseminations was our quota, which were gratefully accepted. I don't know what happened but I think that the ten calves that were born nine months later were the worst bunch of calves we had ever seen — obviously a cock-up somewhere along the line. It was yet another little problem that we could have done without at that time that brings a smile to our faces today. Perhaps the calves were the offspring of some old bull that had escaped the slaughterer's gun!

The police rang one night quite late to say that one of our cows was out on the Brow — panic stations! Torches and everybody up — but it was not one of ours. We did not leave her to roam and we put her in our cow house. I noticed she had not been milked for a couple of days so next morning after we had milked our own, we decided to milk this wandering cow. As Ian started to put the clusters on her teats, all hell was let loose. She literally 'went mad' — lashing out with her feet — a hopeless job. No way was she going to be milked by machine.

Later Gordon Lawrence rang up to ask whether we had seen a spare cow. He described her and I was able to reassure him that his cow was quite all right and tied up in the cow house. She had travelled something like three miles from his farm to ours and the reason she would not be milked by machine was that she was a 'suckler' cow he had brought down from his hill farm somewhere by Glyn Ceiriog as she was producing too much milk for calves to suckle. She had wondered off to look for her calf that had been left up at the hill farm. This one proved the point that suckler cows are never milked by machine.

Chapter 18

Change of Life Style!

AS I write my memories of Foot and Mouth, I often wonder what my life would have been like if we had not gone down. I am sure my daughter would have stayed at home to farm but after the loss of our cows and pigs, Valerie never bothered with farming again. She lost all interest, left school at sixteen and was away to work in Barclay's Bank in Oswestry (Mr. Gwyn Williams was the manager). She stayed for a while before moving to Shrewsbury. She was promoted to the relief team for Shropshire and North Wales and after that became the first woman ever to be in charge of Barclay's Bank at Buckley.

Banking can have its problems and I remember when she came home from work at a bank in North Wales where she had been sent as relief. This area is predominantly Welsh-speaking but my daughter, the only relief available at the time is not a Welsh-speaker. Unfortunately, two or three ladies who used that bank found this out and made it their business to make my daughter's stay there as uncomfortable as they could by repeatedly going to her till and, speaking in their native tongue, asking for a pound's worth of pennies in Welsh or asking what their balance was — always in Welsh. I believe they did this for about three days until Valerie eventually snapped back at one of them and said, 'You will have to wait until a Welsh-speaking girl is available.' The lady took offence and demanded to see the manager. Unfortunately, he did not support Valerie and, I believe, was 'bull-dozed' by the ladies to ring Head Office to report Valerie for insolence and this he did. That night, Valerie arrived home distressed — very upset she was. I think she thought she was going to have the sack. I thought for a moment that perhaps she had 'pinched' some money out of the till — so upset was she.

After she had calmed down and told the full story, I thought for a while, then decided I would deliver Valerie's till keys early next morning. I told her to take the day off and to ring her boss at Shrewsbury and explain what I was doing. Valerie was very loathe to do this or even let me have the keys to her till, but I insisted. Up very early next morning for a journey of nearly forty miles to the bank. It was not yet open so I knocked the door and could hear the locks being undone and bolts sliding back. The door opened about three inches and a voice said, What do you want?'

'A word with the Manager.'

'I am the Manager,' he said.

'Right,' I said, 'First of all, here are the keys to Valerie Strange's till, for which I want a receipt. I am Valerie's father. She will not be in today as she is too upset.' The door opened wider.

'Come in, Mr. Strange,' he said.

'What I've got to say to you can be said on the doorstep,' I said. 'We don't rear girls in Shropshire to come into Wales to be insulted by a small minority of Welsh people, and in my opinion,' I said, 'you did not support a member of your staff who was only doing her job to the best of her ability. You knew that she did not understand Welsh but allowed her, not once, but many times, to be shown up in front of the other staff.'

At that, the telephone rang and as the call was for him, he was required to go. I still stood just outside the door. On the other end of the telephone was Valerie's boss from Head Office. I believe the local man was given a fair 'rollicking' from the Head Manager for his handling of the situation. The Manager came back to me and said in a very subdued voice how sorry he was and he wished that Valerie had come into work as Thursday was pay day for a large factory in the area and it was Valerie's job to pay out the wages.

77

I said, 'You should have thought of that yesterday when you were agreeing with the people who were taking Valerie to task. I still require a receipt for the keys.' This was duly handed over.

'Goodbye,' I said, 'I am going back to Shropshire now as I have horses to shoe and I wouldn't have a job like yours at any price!'

When I arrived home, Valerie was all smiles. She had phoned her boss and he fully backed her — and gave her the rest of the week off with full pay!

A little sequel which I still think sad was that that particular manager somehow managed to get into a financial mix-up at the bank and ended up losing his job. I wonder if the people he supported ever gave him help — I doubt it. What this story has to do with blacksmithing or farming, I don't know — but it shows another facet of one's life. I would imagine that every other father in the same position would have done the same.

Chapter 19

I'm Sorry, Perthy

ABOUT this time, I took the decision to knock down my old Smithy at the Perthy and if I had the chance to redeem my action, now I would not hesitate to do so. How I wish I had listened to older people of the village who said to me that the Old Smithy WAS Welsh Frankton's heritage — but what is heritage to a young person who has a living to make and a family to rear? The old Smithy had served its purpose and was in a bad state of repair. The economics of farming at that time required a different type of blacksmith. Agricultural engineers were the new breed. We acquired an electric welder — drawbars instead of shafts had been the order of the day for years. So, the old Smithy had to go — knocked down unceremoniously with a bulldozer.

North Shropshire District Council's policy insisted that one wall had to be left. The order of the day was to build on the old foundation. I wanted to build about ten yards further back from the road to leave a good drive-in for the bigger farm implements to save parking on the road. But common-sense was not to prevail and the rules had to be obeyed to the letter. This has caused many parking problems, then and since. I acquired a much better workshop — able to shoe horses in and also room to get a tractor and its various attachments under cover — but it has no character, just four straight walls and an asbestos roof. There are no old fashioned wooden shutters to let in the light — just plastic sheets in the roof and electric strip lights. Also gone are the bellows to blow up the old fire with its old-fashioned hearth that I had sat around as a youngster with many other village lads and lasses, roasting potatoes, chestnuts, toasting stale bread scrounged from my mother. It was quite usual on Friday nights to have at least a dozen or so village lads and lasses enjoying the so-called 'treats'. Were they the Macdonalds of yesteryear?

How I wish, as I sit writing here on a winter night, that I had not knocked down our little old Smithy. How I wish it was still here, with all its memories! I vowed I would reconcstruct a village Smithy on my farm and although this has taken some 30 years, at last I have achieved that wish. Little did I think what dramatic changes my life would have but a lot more about that later.

Work was building up in my Smithy at the end of the sixties. More and more horses were starting to re-appear in the area which literally meant that I was back to full-time shoeing of horses, my real love. This also meant employing more labour on the farm which was very difficult at that time. As I have said earlier, men did not want to work at weekends, milking cows when they could get as much in wages working only five days a week in factories — soon to become four and a half days, and three weeks' holiday to boot!

Chapter 20

Brow Farm Goes Accredited

A DECISION taken one Saturday afternoon in my cow house would again bring a dramatic change to my life. We were, by now fully re-stocked. It was 1970 and we were milking sixty cows, and had seventeen in-calf heifers, ten to twelve yearlings and a few calves — something like the same number as before the Foot and Mouth outbreak. Dick Fox was the vet's name who worked for George Wyse. He had come to do a veterinary job to one of the cows and as we were talking, he asked: 'Alf have you had an accredited test on your herd?'

'An accredited test?' I said, 'These cattle have only been here a couple of years or so. These are cattle from other farms all over the country.'

'Well,' he said, 'I strongly advise you to have a test on them. You will have to sooner or later, as before long, all cattle will have to be accredited Brucellosis-free.'

'O.K.' I said. 'I'll leave it with you.'

'We'll do it one day next week,' he said, 'I'll give you a ring to tell you the day I am coming.'

An 'accredited' test means a drop of blood is taken individually from each cow in a herd with a syringe, kept in a separate plastic tube and sent to the Ministry. Each cow is individually tested for Brucellosis. About a week later, Dick Fox came with the results of the test and I can still remember his first words to me, 'You are in trouble and the trouble is . . .'

(I thought he was going to say that the majority of my cows were positive or reactors.) — but no, the other way round.

'Only three showed positive — all the rest were clear. My

81

advice to you is to get rid of those three reactors immediately becasue if one of them aborts, there is a great possibility that the others will too.'

(Abortion means that cows mis-carry long before they are due to calve. It is a terrible tragedy to farmers, — the loss of milk production and loss of condition in the cow. Abortion has been known to ruin many farmers.)

The three were immediately separated from the rest of the herd and a cattle dealer bought them next day for a lot less than I had paid for them. They were three of my best cows. However, that decision was right because, after another three clear tests, nine months later, Brow Farm had an accredited herd, worth a great deal more money. I believe I am right in saying that we were one of the first five herds in Shropshire to become accredited. The Village Blacksmith of Welsh Frankton had become an 'accredited' farmer!

I felt like shouting it from the top of the Brow to let everyone know but decided to keep my secret. I am glad I did because much later, a few years in fact, one of the 'high-flying' farmers of the area told me he had just become accredited. I was able to tell him that I had been accredited for five years, in fact was one of the first five herds in Shropshire. The look on his face gave me a real lift and a sort of glow came all over me.

During this period of my life, things were going along fairly smoothly — well, as smoothly as can be in Farming and Black-smithing — no bank manager to worry about or corn merchant travellers calling. They were more worried about getting an order for corn than miethering about their cheque.

I had sold six heifers to a Co-operative Society Farm whose policy was to pay out their bills at the end of the following month, a delay of possibly six or seven weeks.

At about this time, I was due to visit the bank manager over a few matters, though not by then needing financial help from him, for the first time in about 30 years, even having money tucked away in a Building Society.

However, in passing I did mention the pending transaction, and asked whether I ought to put a bit in my current account as Malcolm Jones was looking for about another 10 heifers to put to the bull to keep the business of buying young heifers and selling them 18 months later as calving or calved heifers, turning over.

The manager advised me not to bother to do that, but that we would have another chat when he returned from a month's cruise.

About a fortnight later, Malcolm arrived with ten or so grand bulling heifers. A deal was struck and I made out a cheque which would have put me about £300 in the red, but the Co-op cheque would put me well in credit again once it arrived.

A week later, I received a letter from the bank telling me and I quote 'not to issue any more cheques' until I had contacted them. Picking up the telephone immediately after reading it twice, I managed to get hold of the writer to ask his authority to write such a letter. He said that when he dictated it, he was acting manager. On further questioning, I found he was only No. 3 and was in charge merely because the No. 2 had gone to a funeral.

I told him in no uncertain terms what I thought of him, and before putting down the telephone told him to have all my policies etc. ready for collection at 10 a.m. the following day, as I was closing my account with his bank.

'What bank are you going to', he asked in a sarcastic voice.

'None of your business. Just do as you are told and get my stuff ready for the morning.' I said.

I think he thought I was bluffing, but I picked up the telephone to ring another bank, asking to speak to Mr. Owen Williams. After a very short discussion, he told me that from 10 a.m. next day, my account would be transferred to his bank, and I would not need to do any more. He would contact my bank and tell them the position.

At about 10.30 that day, the No. 3 at my old bank rang, asking me to change my mind and stay with them until the manager returned. 'When you were sitting in your ivory tower choosing to write to me, you could not even wait for the No. 2 to return from a funeral before doing so. I have been laughed at long enough by people like you, who on reflection are only little fish in a very big sea', I told him.

This whole sequence really started with the selling of heifers to the Co-op but once again there was a sequel. A phone message from the farm manager informed me that one of them was light in one quarter, though he had kept her a month without telling me.

He was however adamant he was only going to pay me for the other five. I thought it no use arguing and made arrangements for Syd Downe's to pick up the heifer the following day. I rang next morning to make sure the farm manager had obtained an Accredited Movement Certificate.

He said his farm was not Accredited. I dare not repeat my reply, for here was a man prepared to send a non-Accredited heifer back to my farm. Had he been allowed to do so I would have lost my Accredited Licence. Had he not told me he was not Accredited, I wonder what price his job was worth and he would probably be summonsed by the Ministry of Agriculture as well.

I fetched the heifer from his farm and took her straight to Don Wynn's Hadley Farm. I knew he was looking for some Accredited heifers, but as he himself was not yet fully Accredited, moving my one heifer there was O.K.

The farm manager paid all expenses and another £50 for me for all the hassle. If I had reported him to the ministry, who knows what the outcome would be.

Changing banks was one of the best day's work I ever did, for with encouragement from Owen and a little help from the bank, I became the proud owner of Brow Farm. Owen became a firm friend and we have enjoyed many games of golf together as well as the odd liquid lunch together arranged by his secretary, Sinah Davies.

Chapter 21

Ian and the Herd

OUT of the blue, Ian, my cowman for the last ten years, decided he wanted to go to Denmark to work.

'I don't know' I said to him, 'Go for three months and if you don't like their country, come back and your job will still be here.'

I thought I could stand on my head for three months by employing relief milkers — but no, he was adamant — he wanted to go to Denmark. However, he was very good. He gave me three months to sort things out. What to do? I didn't know — no chance of another cowman. They were like gold. Then again — a stroke of luck — an advert in the *Farmer's Weekly* or was it the *Farmer and Stockbreeder* (I can't remember):

'Wanted — a herd of sixty to eighty milkers. Must be accredited.' All it gave was a phone number. It could have been Scotland or London for all I knew. But believe me, or believe me not, it was Wrexham — less than fourteen miles away — Pontrochen Farms Ltd., a Mr. Arthur Jones. His son, Alan had bought a farm less than five miles from me and that's where they wanted the cows for — unbelievable! — Ebnal Farm, Rhosagadfa. I rang the number and an appointment was made for them to view the cows at Brow Farm next day. Mr. Jones came with his two sons, stayed about an hour looking at the cows and heifers. A price was agreed on the complete herd of sixty cows and fifteen in-calf heifers, a shake of the hand, and the deal was struck — the complete disposal of a life time's work in under an hour. Only one other thing to be agreed — could I look after them for another month or so as their milking set up would not be ready for a month.

It turned out to be nearer two months but as there was no 'luck' money given, I agreed my part of the bargain would be the looking after Alan's cows, see to the calving of them (day or night). One of the biggest worries I have ever had is looking after someone else's cows and I remember so well the first cow to calve. I lost the calf over calving — a good start! However, that one was the only one I lost over about twenty calvings.

Then came the day to move the cows five miles away — cows which had been used to being tied up with cow chains in a cow house were suddenly moved to loose housing and then had to go through a small doorway to be milked on what was called a 'Roundabout' milking set up. What a shock to the cows! They literally had to be 'manhandled' individually through the door way on to the Roundabout. The cows were moved on the Saturday and for the first day, it required about six people to be there at milking times to help. In less than a week, they were following one aonther in as if they had been milked in this way all their life.

I have often thought about that sale of mine — two country people and a lot of money involved. By today's standard, about £80,000 on the shake of a hand — but a lot of trust both ways. Country dealing again at its best. Over the years, I have often wondered on the use of accountants, but on previous advice from Bernard Hallett my herd had been placed on 'Herd' basis — meaning that once in a life time you can sell your milking herd, thereby not attracting full tax.

In my second book *Following Me Dad* I mentioned a certain Mr. Mackie's boat, named the *Duchess Countess* Mrs. Crowe nee Marjery Samspon has supplied me with a much fuller version.

Mr. Mackie's boat, was built over a century and a half ago. It was one of the Duke of Bridgewater's original packet boats — the name of the craft recalls the titles in the Bridgewater family.

The *Duchess Countess,* in her hey-day, conveyed passengers

86

at the rate of a penny a mile between Stockton Quay and Manchester, the return journey occupying thirteen hours.

Having a beam of six feet, she was long enough to accomodate thirty passengers together with their goods, and a day's refreshments.

The *Duchess Countess* had a crew of three, the captain, the mate, — the 'jockey', and she was drawn by relays of four horses. Boats travelling from Manchester claimed the right of way over those approaching the city, but aristocratic *Duchess Countess* had the right of way in either direction. To demonstrate her superior status she carried a large 'S' shaped knife at her bows. If any boatman contested her right of way, his towrope was promptly severed. It has been recorded that there were occasions when passengers were 'seasick' aboard her. With the development of railways, and the conveyance of passengers became uneconomic, the once proud *Duchess Countess* was demoted to the menial job of carrying cattle and poultry into Manchester, returning with cargoes of fustian. In 1915 the old craft did her last regular voyage, and was taken to Runcorn, where she was scuttled with other boats in the Big Pool.

After being submerged there for 18 years, she was refloated, and used by her new owner for exploring the Shropshire Union and neighbouring canals. For some years he kept her moored close to the small dock at Lower Frankton and from there made trips in different directions — a favourite one being over the Welsh border to cross the famous aquaducts at Chirk and Froncysyllte. The *Duchess Countess* was also the last boat to navigate the Montgomery Canal before it was closed.

During the war years the old boat began to leak badly, and repair work being then out of the question, a team of willing villages dragged her out on the canal bank, in the field of Mr. Tom Lewis. The site is rather a lonely one, but Mr. Mackie was never envious of those living in more elaborate surroundings. A small range served for heating and cooking, light as obtained by means of an oil lamp, and a wireless provided news of the outside world, together with a collection of well chosen books, for he was a very well read man. His adventures included fishing unfortunates out of the canal and when an infuriated bull got a horn wedged in the ironwork. I cannot remember where the boat went after preservation, or the date of the old gentleman's demise.

Chapter 22

The Old Black Sow

A HEAVY fall of snow greeted us on the morning of 6th January, 1968. Roads up the Perthy were impassable to cars. Only tractors could get through. Wal Powell, a bricklayer lived at No. 5 Higher Perthy — no work for him that day — but somehow or other he had to get to Ellesmere with a prescritpion for his father in law, Fred Edwards, who lived with him. Fred's home was in Lower Frankton but not being too well and his wife having passed away, he was staying with Marie, his daughter.

Wal decided to walk the two and a half miles to Ellesmere to the chemists. He did this in the morning and after picking up the tablets, decided to go around to one of his mates for a cup of tea. The cup of tea turned into a drinking session with a couple of mates who had called around (remember — too much snow and frost for them to work?) After consuming all the leftovers from Christmas, they went to another mate's house to finish off his as well. Then, against their better judgement, they decided to go and drink the White Hart pub dry as well. This, after another two hours, proved beyond them.

By now, Wallace was feeling a little the worse for wear but not to be out done, struck off for home — two and a half miles away. By now, the main road was passable to traffic and luckily for Wal, my brother Jack was coming home in a Water Board van, having difficulty in passing Wal, who seemed to require more than his share of the road. They managed to get him into the van and brought him to the Brow Farm, where I now live. The lane from Brow Farm to Wal's house is very narrow and very dark but Wal insisted he would be able to negotiate the last five hundred yards without further help from Jack. Jack pointed him down the lane, knowing there would be no traffic at least.

Our phone had rung about two hours earlier. Dr. Mike Elder rang to ask a favour. His father, Tommy Elder, who lived in a bungalow on The Ridge was a bit low on bread and butter. The Ridge is about half a mile from the Brow.

As Mr. Elder was unable to get out himself, I was happy to oblige, for because of the heavy fall of snow, we on the main road, were better placed to get out. My daughter, Valerie, decided to come with me for a walk. We delivered the bread and butter to Tommy Elder and after a drink and a warm, made our way back home. It was nearly dark, when we arrived at the entrance to the little dark lane, Valerie leading — when, all of a sudden, half way along the lane, she stopped in her tracks.

'What's the matter?' I enquired.

'Dad, it looks like the old black sow.'

The shape moving along towards us did look like the old black sow but on closer inspection, I realised it was Wal, in his dark donkey jacket. He had decided he could make better progress home on his hands and knees. Apparently, he was having great difficulty in staying upright on his feet. I managed to get his hands around my shoulders to keep him upright and progressed towards his home, Wal protesting all the way that he was fully capable of getting home without my assistance.

We were met by the gate by Marie who enquired in a not too gentle voice what had taken him so long to get the tablets (which as luck would have it, he had not lost). Before Marie could turn on me. I assured her that I had only just met Wal in the lane. We got him into the house and I thought that 'retreat' was the best thing to do so — we quickly 'did a bunk'.

They had been happily married for twenty eight years but I believe that in the next hour or two, the marriage did have a rough time. Many is the laugh over the years we have all had together over another episode in the life of the village. This year, the story came up again when I was asked to propose a toast at their Golden Wedding — Fifty happy years and still living on the Perthy in the same house — we hope for many more years.

The black sow mentioned was tragically slaughtered in the Foot and Mouth epidemic of 1967 at Brow Farm. Wal was for five years in the S.A.S. of the 1939-45 war. (The Special Air Service) Today, despite a touch of rheumatism, he walks with a stick, and can still make a good glass of all types of wine — carrot is my favourite and by accident or deliberate design, when Marie had her usual Mothers' Union fete, somehow or other, Wal's strong best carrot wine was used instead of Marie's weaker apple juice. The draw and proceeds of her little fete were a record — and a good time was had by all!

Chapter 23

Goose and Hot Cross Buns

ABOUT this time, I was having a game of golf with Ted Hollywell, owner of one of the leading furniture stores in Oswestry. He had bought a property at Hengoed with about an acre of land which he did not want to farm. He asked the best way to keep down the grass and I suggested rather than have sheep which require a certain amount of attention, the next best thing was a couple of geese (a goose and gander), allowing them to breed naturally and when he had got about seven or eight, they would eat as much as a cow, and the grass would be kept nice and short — no mowing required.

This Ted did but tragedy struck. One goose after another vanished — something was taking them. Ted realised desperate measures were required as he was now down to one goose and suspected a fox was doing the damage.

So he set a trap to catch the fox, fitting up large floodlights to light up the field — connected to a switch in his garage close by. Arming himself with a twelve bore gun and a bottle of Scotch to keep out the cold and give him courage and with a blanket to keep him warm, he settled down to wait for the victim.

The old fox was lothe to appear as night went into morning and the liquid in the bottle was fast disappearing — when, all of a sudden — action stations!

On went the floodlights and the sight that greeted his eyes was of the fox having grabbed the goose and, as they do, throwing it up in the air and catching it on the way down. Taking careful aim through glazed eyes, Ted fired — missed the fox but tragically shot the goose instead. The fox escaped into the night and Ted still can't remember whether he finished the bottle that night — another true country story that needed recording.

On Easter Saturday around 1970 Morris's van of Shrewsbury was driven into our farm yard. The driver, Ron Kidgel used to live on the Perthy but had moved to Shrewsbury with his job. He came into the Blacksmith's Shop and said, 'Do you want any hot cross buns?'

'I don't know,' was my reply. 'I expect Vera has bought some.'

'No, I don't want to sell them. Do you want them for the pigs? It's a cancelled order and they are two days old so they have to be dumped — they'll be alright for the pigs.'

After I had looked at them, I said, 'They're too good for the pigs.'

'It's up to you what you do with them, I have to get rid of them,' said Ron.

We cleaned off our kitchen table which was eight feet long and four feet wide (one side leaned against the wall). I was expecting about four or five dozen but tray after tray full kept coming in until the table was full and the pile stretched up the wall, until it looked like half a roof of hot cross buns. I have never in my life seen so many — there must have been hundreds.

'Cheerio,' said Ron. 'Enjoy your tea!'

'What are you going to do with them?' said Vera.

I was lost for words. Then I had a brain wave. 'Get Valerie and Alan a big basket each and they can take them full up the Perthy and give each household a couple of dozen. But after half of Welsh Frankton had had a share, there was still a tableful of reasonably fresh hot cross buns. Miss Annie Clay came for water from our tap as she did not have mains water. 'Go and fetch a basket,' said Vera, 'I'll give you some hot cross buns.' Vera filled her basket with the buns and when it was nearly full, Miss Clay said, 'Oh, that'll do Mrs. Strange. No, no, you'll rob yourself!' There were still the best part of two hundred buns on the table. I have never been so sick of hot cross buns because for most of that week we had hot cross buns every meal time in different forms, toasted with jams on to change the taste, bread pudding every day for a week, and custards with buns baked in them. Towards the end of the week, what was left was fed to the pigs. I have never been so glad to get back to a normal diet. I am sure I saw a smile on the dog's face!

Chapter 24

George Pryke and His Lad

GEORGE PRYKE, the gamekeeper I mentioned earlier, came to work as gamekeeper to Major Kynaston in 1923 after war service and has lived in his cottage ever since. This year, we hope he will celebrate his 100th birthday in December 1993 — 71 years on the same estate — 71 years a gamekeeper and the longest surviving keeper and still working. There are so many stories to tell of George but my favourite is this one. I had suffered a major heart attack in October 1980 — it was bad — — but more of that later. In April 1981, I took my first walk to my beloved Hardwicke Pool, about half a mile from home. I had a portable telephone with me in case I needed to summon help from Vera. I had a good look at the pool, 'drinking in' the sight of that beautiful stretch of water — a scene I never thought I would see again — and slowly made my way home up the big field, stopping for the occasional rest. All of a sudden, a voice asked, 'How are you, Alf?'

It was George and before I had time to answer, he said, 'I can't stop to talk. All the birds have escaped out of their pens and I am going to get my lad to give me a hand to get them back in.'

His 'lad' was Windsor Taylor who had come as a gamekeeper to take over from George but as George had not retired, he was still the 'lad'! This was in 1981, George was 87, and the 'lad', Windsor, 71. Sadly, Windsor passed away about ten years later, leaving George still as head keeper — as he is to this day.

I cannot vouch for the truth of the story that George recently told the Colonel he would soon be due for another new suit (a country tradition whereby the landlord buys his gamekeeper a new suit). Long may you live, George — so many happy memories I have of you — I suppose if you had been paid for all your hours' work, you would be a millionaire.

Today's so-called 'gamekeepers' in their four-wheel drive vehicles to go around the woods in my opinion, are not in the same league. George had his birds in the woods. Today, they are all over the place, A true sign of a good gamekeeper is birds in the woods, not being run over on the roads.

Ten years ago, I went to the President's Cricket Match on Hardwicke Park. With me was my twelve-months old grandson, and enjoying a drink with George, then 89. He said, 'Alf, I don't suppose I will live long enough to run your grandson around Hardwicke Woods,' but you see the uncertainty of life. My grandson is now 11 and George coming up to 100. Only a few years ago, he had a bad 'turn' and was taken into hospital. After a couple of days, he signed himself out. How wonderful for him to have had such good health apart from failing eyesight.

George Pryke, about whom I have written many stories has now reached the magic figure of 100 years old. He was guest of honour at two parties in celebration of the fact (see picture) of a cricket bat presented by my brothers Bill and Jack on behalf of Frankton Cricket Club. George was a member for 75 years.

His nephew Dave Pryke called to see him a couple of days before his 100th birthday and invited him to go for a meal to the Narrowboat Inn, George declined the offer saying he could not spare the time as they were shooting at Hardwick Hall the next day and he wanted to be around the woods that afternoon.

Sadly George has since passed away five weeks after his 100th birthday. And a sign of the times we now live in sadly while George's relations and his many friends were at his funeral in Welsh Frankton Church, some mindless moron broke into and burgled his country cottage. Words fail me.

The Shropshire County Junior 1974.
Back row, left to right: Alan Strange, Peter Martin, Sandy Lyle and Mike Simcock.
Front row, left to right: Philip Gee, Richard Green, Ian Woosnam and Alan Lewis with organiser
Alan Hargreave.

Snowball – the stew eating pony.

William Ryder's Headstone.

Standing: Bill Strange.   *Seated left to right:* Alf, George and Jack.
(Since writing this book George Pryke has sadly passed away exactly
five weeks after his 100th birthday.)
                    By kind permission of David Harris.

Rescuing six heifers from the frozen Hardwicke Pool.

A presentation was made to Ellesmere firemen of an R.S.P.C.A. Certificate of Merit, for rescuing six heifers from the frozen Hardwicke Pool, Welsh Frankton. Five of the heifers survived. The presentation was made by H.M. Inspector of Fire Services, Mr. L. O. Clarke at the Ellesmere station. The six members who took part in the rescue are (from left), Fireman S. D. Harris, Leading Fireman J. W. Butler, Fireman W. R. Kynaston, Fireman H. T. Stone, Leading Fireman S. Deakin and Fireman P. R. Wilson.

A typical scene at the time of the Foot and Mouth disease.

Hamish and Richard Foster – September 1982

Ray Nicholls – Derwen Student.

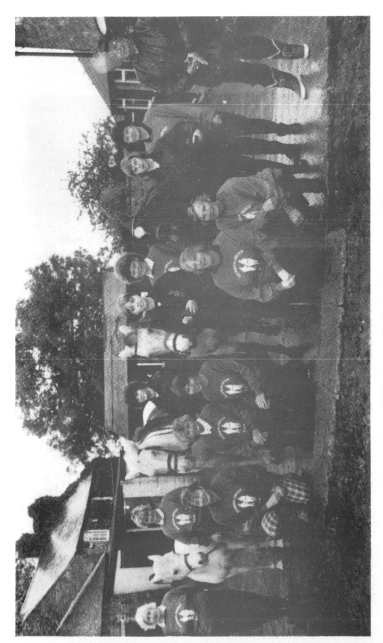

Derwen Group Riding for the Disabled with students and helpers.

Ron Jones, Wal Powell and Alf Strange – one rabbit less!!

Barry Woolham and Alf Strange 'going for their morning ride'.

Four Grandsons.

Grandchildren

From left to right: Helen Strange (16 months); Joseph Jones (11); Robert Strange ($4\frac{1}{2}$);
Thomas Jones (9); David Strange (6).

Chapter 25

A Christmas Pint

THE mention of Tom Glassy Jones Brumeck? brings a groan to Norm and Alex Birch, brother Jack and myself. Tom Jones was the farmer's name. 'Glassy' was his nickname. Well, he brought a Brumeck to the Smithy one day. It needed welding and a new handle putting on. A Brumeck is what you have to lay hedges with.

Christmas Eve, 1953 was the night in question. Norman, Alex, Jack and I had gone to the Market Hotel in Ellesmere for our usual Christmas drink and who was there but Tom Glassy Jones who farmed at Birch Hill. He shouted across, 'How much do I owe you for mending my Brumeck?' 'I'll see you in a minute,' I said, ordering our drinks and preparing to pay for them. Fred Davies, the landlord at the time, said, 'Those are paid for by Tom.'

Wishing Tom all the best, we drank our pints. I suppose the round would have cost under ten shillings (50p today) equal, I suppose, to the cost of repairing a Brumeck and new stale. We all paid our turn and the time to go home arrived.

Tom said, 'I anna paid you for the Brumeck.' I said, 'You bought a round of drinks so that's about right.'

'Not likely!' said Tom. 'Here Fred, four large Scotches for these lads.'

'No,' we said. 'We've had our quota for tonight.'

But to no avail, The drinks were already served and against our better judgment, we drank the large Scotches. In those days, working lads did not drink whisky — a luxury drink. It was for older and wealthier men. Norman and Freda lived at

Tetchill at that time. Alex was staying overnight at Norman's with his wife Brenda and their little daughter, Julie. The story goes that Alex could not play his 'Father Christmas' part. He fell up the stairs, waking up his daughter, Julie at an unearthly time of the morning and I believe I'm also right that he had a difficult job facing breakfast and Christmas dinner the next day!

Whenever I see Alex, who himself is now retired, we always say 'Let's have one on the Brumeck.' I say yet again, was it really 42 years ago?

Melvyn Gough, Doug Gough's youngest son, was learning to drive. Now, 'What has that to do with Jack Powell from Criftins bike?' you may wonder — but it does have a lot to do with it. Melvyn had been helping us to harvest on a Saturday afternoon. We finished about eight o'clock in the evening — quick wash and change and away to the Fox Inn at Criftins, Melvyn driving his dad's car which he parked quite close to a hedge. We went for a couple of pints (harvesting is a thirsty job — manhandling bales with no elevator on our farm!) We did not stay long as we were going for some fish and chips at Sal Chadwicks' up St. John's Hill. Doug elected to drive — pulled the starter of the car (it started immediately) and reversed a couple of yards — straight over Jack Powell's bike! The car had been left in reverse when Melvyn parked it. Calamity — Doug 'went over' Melvyn for leaving the car in reverse gear but the damage was done — no good falling out. Jack Powell had to be fetched to be told what had happened to his beloved bike — his only means of transport.

After surveying the damage, Jack enquired of Doug what he was going to do about it (the bike, I mean). Doug made him a good offer and said, 'I'll bring you my own bike, which is newer than yours. I'll bring it over tomorrow.' Jack agreed.

However, next day when he arrived at Jack's with a very good bike and said, 'There you are Mr. Powell. You have a very good bargain. My new bike for your old one.'

'What do you mean?' said Jack. 'You inna having my bike as well. I'm keeping that!' After a long discussion, Jack eventually accepted the new and better bike and Doug had his old and battered bike to repair — he needed a bike himself.

Every good story has a sequel and this came about a week later, again after harvesting. We went to the Fox for a drink. As Doug went through the door into the bar, Jack Powell was playing dominoes and not known as a man to mince his words, he called out, 'Mr. Gough, I want the saddle off my old bike as this saddle of yours is rubbing my bloody arse raw!' The locals roared with laughter. However, a swap of saddles was arranged for the following Saturday.

Quite recently, I acquired Doug's old bike to put in my old collection of bikes — complete with a good saddle! On it, will be placed a small plaque to say it is the one to which another little bit of country history was attached.

Over the years, we have often had a laugh about an incident that happened thirty years ago.

Chapter 26

Pitcher to the Well

WORKING at a local farm one day, around 1970, welding handles to go on to a wall a local builder was building. I believe he had been at the farm for some time on different jobs and to say that the farmer's wife would have made a church warden or a deaconess of a chapel would have been a serious untruth. She, as I remember, could 'cuss a bit'.

Apparently, the builder, or his men, had been responsible for breaking, over the previous weeks, about three pitcher jugs in which she had brought them tea. This particular afternoon, she brought it in a large enamel tea jug, put it on the wall and told the builders, 'There, break that b . . . . !'

After drinking their tea, one of the workers removed it off wall, saying, 'I'll put it somewhere safe — in the door way of the cow house.'

Soon, a wagon arrived with a load of bricks, made a three point turn in the yard, and to everyone's dismay, backed over the new enamel jug, flattening it like a pancake.

Finishing my welding job double quick, I made a speedy get-away. I believe that when the lady came for her jug, the cursing and raising of her voice could be heard in Whittington. Whether they had any more jugs of tea, I cannot say.

Chapter 27

'Me Wobbler's Gone

AFTER the Foot and Mouth epidemic, quite a few farmers went out of milk production or in many cases, did not restock for many different reasons. In some cases, the age of the farmer who required a more leisurely life style. In some cases, buildings required repair to bring premises up to the standard required as new regulations were being imposed on farms. In some cases, the bank had grabbed the whole of their compensation cheques and they could not afford to re-stock.

All this was bringing more work to the blacksmith. This brings me to a farmer in the area who decided to go out of milk and plough his farm up for corn. It was a grass farm and most of his fields were not suitable for corn growing — but plough it all up he did. As bad luck would have it, I think it was one of the wettest summers on record which meant his machines constantly became bogged down. He also had problems with the clapped-out combine he had bought second-hand having seen better days and many summers of hard work on other farms.

I had been to repair it at least twice a week from about the middle of August. One Sunday afternoon about the middle to the end of October, when I had already made the usual two visits to weld and repair it that week, we agreed that for the following year he would have to buy himself a better harvester. 'If you can keep her going,' he said, 'for just a bit longer, I will pension her off.'

I was in the farm yard at the Brow on this particular Sunday afternoon and had promised Vera that we would go for a ride

101

once I had finished a little job off — but calamity was to strike. I can seen Vera coming up the yard with a downcast look on her face. So-and-so is on the phone and wants a word with you.

'Hello,' I said, 'What's your problem?'

'Alf,' he said, 'Me Wobbler's gone now.'

'Oh dear,' I said, 'Mine went years ago.'

'Oh,' he said. 'I didna know you had a combine. What make is her?'

(To non-farming readers, a 'Wobbler' is a part of a combine that shakes the corn out the head of the corn, called the *hulls*.)

As I did not stock wobblers, it was next day before I could get the old combine going. Next year a better combine was acquired, that did not require so many repairs.

In about 1967, before Foot and Mouth, soon after coming to Brow Farm, Saturday mornings were always busy. Bill Hodnett came to give us a hand on the farm, attending to the odd blocked drain or laying hedges. That is a skilled job — as is putting a barbed wire fence up (it must be tight in between the posts otherwise it is no good at all) and hanging a field gate. Bill could do all those types of jobs but could not drive a tractor.

But he could plough a straight furrow with a pair of horses and one Saturday morning, Alan, my son, then about eight years old had been with Bill to put up some barbed wire. When they came in for dinner, Alan whispered to me, 'Bill is a wise man.' He had shown Alan how to tighten barbed wire!

To those who don't know it, Brow Farm is situated on the top of a long, steep hill, and if a tractor would not start, it was quite a simple job to run her down the Brow. If she had not started by the time you got to the bottom of the Brow, you were in trouble.

Come Saturday morning, a tractor with the muck spreader hooked to it was stuck at the bottom of the Brow. Ian came back for help with another tractor which was just as awkward to start as the one at the bottom of the Brow, which had a fertiliser drill attached.

We hooked to the other tractor, which meant we had two

tractors, a fertiliser spreader and a muck spreader in a row — could have been fifty feet or more in length.

Now, I am not the best of tractor drivers and I really don't know what happened, but my foot slipped off the clutch and managed to stall the towing tractor — calamity! This meant borrowing another tractor and starting again.

I did not realise how many farmers had seen our problem until later when we had numerous phone calls over the next few days, enquiring — 'Are you moving Alf?' 'Does the Bank Manager know?' and 'Pity you sold the horse!' It's to be hoped that sort of country leg-pulling and humour continues and we shall always be able to laugh at trivial episodes like that — not funny at the time but which thirty years on, raise a ready smile.

We had re-seeded a twenty acre field the modern way by spraying with 'Roundup' (killing all the old grass and weeds) and directly re-seeding with grass. A good job was done by the contractors and quite good grass established. Unfortunately, an abundance of daisies came up with the ley. Advice from Bill Hall of ADAS was asked for and he said, 'Don't spray as they are only one year's daisies. Give them a good hard grazing, then top them with a good topper and you will have a first class ley. Mind you,' he added, 'they will look a bit of a mess for a month or two but if you can stand the leg-pulls, all will be well.' John Clay grazed and topped them for me but before that, people were slowing up and asking whether it was some special mixture I was growing. 'Is it something for horses?'

For a week or two, the field was really pretty — thousands of daisies — but the classic was the night George Edwards called and enquired from Vera if he could have a few flowers for the church on Sunday! — which reminds me of the piece of poetry, 'The Field Next to the Road'.

Chapter 28

Miss Salter's Riding Crop

THE early 1970s was a period when I was building up the shoeing of horses again, though I was reaching fifty — a time of life when you should be starting to slow down a bit. I seemed to be working very long hours including Saturdays and Sundays. A shortage of farriers was apparent but this particular incident brought home to me that there is more to life than making money.

It is one of the nicest things that ever happened to me. Every Thursday afternoon through the winter months, from the end of October to the middle of March, I used to play golf with Don Wyn, a farmer friend from Hadley Farm, Whitchurch — in younger days, a county rugby player, as was also, his son, John (one of the few fathers and sons who played together for Whitchurch).

As usual, Thursday morning was a bit hectic in getting work finished in order to get to Oswestry Golf Club for about one o'clock. The last cup of coffee and butty and lacing up shoes was always done with one eye on the clock — when Vera said, 'Miss Salter is coming across the road.' 'I can't stop to talk to her now,' was my reply. 'I am late so I'll go up the backyard and give her the slip.'

My Mini Van was in the back and as always loaded with horse shoes, smithy tack, and golf clubs piled on top of them. I was about to take off, when Vera appeared, 'You can't go, Miss Salter has run out of petrol at the bottom of the Brow' (about half a mile away on a very fast stretch of the main road).

'Where is she now?' I enquired.

'Waiting by the front door,' was her reply.

I uttered a few oaths that would not have pleased my Sunday School teacher and got out of my van, knowing I had no petrol in a can. The last gallon had been used the day before for someone else. Miss Salter was a rather frail dear old lady, well into her eighties.

'You get her across the main road,' I said to Vera, 'and I will get some petrol from Fred's garage.'

By the time I got back, Miss Salter was the right side of the road for me to pick her up. I literally lifted her unceremoniously on to the passenger seat — scarcely enough room for her — a good job she had a hat pin in her hat as I'm sure it wobbled and nearly came off. We proceeded at great speed to her car — a beautiful, immaculate A30 car in British racing green. Miss Salter had left it touching the white line with two wheels and had locked it. By the time she had got the keys out of her handbag, I had put the petrol in her tank. A large lorry whizzed by and I thought the driver was giving us the Churchill 'V' sign in reverse !

'Switch on,' I said to Miss Salter, 'and pull the starter.' This she proceeded to do and to my satisfaction, the car roared into life.

'Cheerio,' I said to Miss Salter. 'I'll see you again some time. I am in a hurry to go.' Life is not as simple as that. She switched the car off and to my amazement, got out and said, 'I must pay you for the petrol.' The furthest thought in my head was Miss Salter wanting to pay for the petrol in the middle of a main road.

'Don't worry about that,' I said. 'Pay Vera or call and pay Fred at the petrol station.'

'No indeed not — I must pay you for it. You've been so kind.' There was no use in arguing. She had a pound note in her hand. Petrol at that time was about 80p. Instead of giving me the pound note which was 20p too much and would perhaps have bought a pint, she started searching her purse but, could only raise 75p.

'That will do,' I said.

'Indeed not,' was her reply — but still held on to her pound note. After further discussion, which seemed to take ages, she eventually agreed to pay Vera at Brow Farm the right money, and get her 20p change!

I could see my game of golf disappearing fast. She eventually got behind the steering wheel, started her motor up again and winding her window down, she then thanked me again, saying what a good fellow I was. Under my breath, I was saying, 'I wish you'd b . . . . . off!'

Eventually, off she went, with me following as I wanted to make sure that she got over the top of the Brow. I am no mechanic but know it is possible to have an air lock in a petrol pipe after running out of petrol. I wanted to make sure she would be all right before going for my belated game of golf.

Arriving at the first tee twenty minutes or so late, Don asked me, 'What made you so late?' My reply was, 'You'll never believe me if I try to tell you. Let's have our game.' This we did, and a drink in the bar afterwards ended my half-day at a very busy time.

Now, one might feel this story is what can happen to thousands of other people and I would agree, but, there was a sequel.

About a month later, arriving home late from shoeing, Vera said, 'There's a present for you on the middle room table.' All wrapped up in Christmas paper was a bone handled hunting crop with an inlaid silver band and a silver disc with a London's firm's name on it. Attached was a little note from Miss Salter, thanking me once again for being so kind to her that day on the Brow when she ran out of petrol, hoping I would accept it with her grateful thanks. I was deeply touched and hung the hunting crop over my old fashioned fireplace at Brow Farm. Miss Salter was over eighty years of age and the hunting crop had been owned by her grandfather.

Six weeks to the day after the first episode, late as usual, I was getting ready for my game — cup of coffee in one hand, butty in the other and trying to lace up shoes at the same time, when Vera remarked, 'Miss Salter is coming to the door.' I thought she must have been joking but she was not. Miss Salter was, in fact, coming to the door. 'Never!' I said. 'She canna have run out of petrol again!'

Leaving Vera to answer the door, I allowed her enough time to catch me up at the backyard. But Miss Salter had not run out of petrol this time. On arriving from my game, Vera said, 'Miss Salter has brought you another present.' This time it was a beautiful leather wallet that she had made for her sister, some eighty years before when she was at school. Inside, were a beautiful pair of gold rimmed spectacles the — clip-on-your-nose type and embossed in the leather were her sister's initials, A.L.S. — Ada Langford Slater. My initials are also A.L.S. — Alfred Leslie Strange so that little leather wallet could be handed down to another generation. The value of the hunting crop I know is in excess of three figures and the little leather wallet? Well, its gold rimmed spectacles are priceless in sentimental value alone.

Alan, my son, is Alan Leslie Strange also.

The hunting crop and the wallet have pride of place over my fireplace and every time I look at them, I feel quite guilty of the way I 'chucked' Miss Salter into my Mini van that Thursday afternoon, many moons ago.

To this particular story, there is even a sequel to a sequel. One afternoon, a gentleman at the door asked Vera where I was. He came into my Smithy and introduced himself as Miss Salter's nephew from America. I told him the two stories about his aunt and when I had finished, he said to me,

'You will never guess my name?'

'No idea,' was my reply.

'Albert Leonard Salter — A.L.S..'

Chapter 29

Nature's Way

IT was in 1947 at Sid Rowe's Smithy near Craven Arms that I passed my exams to be a fully-qualified farrier. In those days, it was a seven-year apprenticeship and after you had passed, you could add three letters after your name, 'R.S.S.' which meant you were a Registered Shoeing Smith. Normally, after a few years, you would go in for a higher exam which was your A.F.C.L. This meant that you became an Asociate Fellow of the College of London. This gave one more of an insight into the surgical side of shoeing and meant one had to be able to make twenty eight different types of surgical shoe, know what they were for and also had to know what exactly happened in a horse's leg from the knee down. Probably many readers do not know that shoeing is a man-made evil. Horses were not intended to be shod and putting on iron shoes causes a lot of problems. One of the most common complaints are corns — yes a horse gets corns! — due mainly to a shoe being left on too long. It invariably happens in hunting horses due to excessive road work and galloping on hard surfaces but if the horse is regularly shod by a good farrier, a long hunting season can often be attained. Of course, there are exceptions which brings me to a case I had a few years ago.

I was by now a fully qualified A.F.C.L., as was my brother, Jack and also the two Handleys (father and son) from Pipe Gate in Stafford. We took our A.F.C.L. at Hereford Training College and passed quite easily after very good expert instruction by Mr. Ted Morris. (In 1947 we took our R.S.S. and thirty years later, we took our A.F.C.L.) Ted was a first class farrier trom the Midlands. As I remember we went for about twelve months, mainly through the winter months — every Thursday night to Ernie Frost's Smithy at Eccleshall. I also remember that the head of instruction at Hereford was Mr. Bill Watts. None of my books has been written as instructional books on farrier's work, they are about people and country characters I have met over the years.

I will just mention a particular instance when my qualification as a farrier was doubted. The horse had been regularly shod by me from about the August ready for cub hunting. It had been bought very recently by this particular farmer, so there was no previous record of the horse. Quite a good season had been had by horse and rider but it was towards the end of the season (late February) when I received a phone call from the owner that his horse was showing signs of lameness. I immediately examined the front feet very carefully — no trace of corns, only a slight bruising to the sole of the foot, not enough to warrant any attention. I remarked that if both horse and rider were to lose a bit of weight, that would help the problem no end.

'Can we go hunting tomorrow?' he asked.

'As far as I am concerned, there is no problem with its feet. See how it goes.'

The next night, in a rather agitated phone call informing me, I was told they had not had a good day's hunting due to the horse not going at all well. It did not seem to want to gallop. The owner informed me he had had the vet who had said that the horse had corns and that I was to shoe the horse. I made the remark there and then on the phone to the owner, 'Your horse has not got corns, and you are wasting your money.' However, he was adamant I was wrong and that the vet was right.

I made a pair of corn shoes and put them on the horse for the owner to go hunting the following Saturday and remarked again about the weight of the horse. He did not ring me on the Saturday night but I had found out from friends in hunting circles that the horse and its owner had again retired early. The horse was unable to gallop for any length of time so — I rang him and asked if the corn shoes had made any difference. The reply was 'Not a bit.'

The horse was still not right so it was decided to rest it for the remainder of the hunting season. (which was nearly over anyway.) I took the shoes off — still no sign of any corns. Then the owner decided to put the mare in foal but after about a month had gone by and many journeys to the stallion, the mare did not want to be put in foal.

The vet who had said that the horse had corns was called out to wash the horse's stomach and inject her so that she would come into season, to produce a foal in about eleven months, the following March. It was still no use.

The mare was determined, despite all that had been done, not to be put in foal. One morning, about a month later, what should be standing in the field but the mare with a fully-fledged foal by her side — both fit and well — no sign of lameness. The mare had been in foal all the time — hence, the lameness two months or so earlier — back to my reasoning at that time to put the mare and the owner on a diet! The vet in question has never mentioned the case to me and I don't think the owner did either — but a wry smile will come to my face when I think that I was right. The reason the poor horse could not gallop was that she was nine months in foal at that time. Nature's way of showing she was in foal had been ignored.

Chapter 30

Friends and Story Tellers

ONE of the most interesting characters it has been my privilege
to know was Noel Reece. I first met him in the seventies as a
member of Oswestry Golf Club and what a delightful man to
know he was. He had a wealth of stories and what a wonderful
story teller he had been in his younger days, I believe. He had
been a school teacher and in the Diplomatic Service in Malaya
before the 1939-45 war. Taken prisoner by the Japanese he
was in their hands for ten years or so. Many are the stories he
told me of his interment, the majority of which, I do not
intend to repeat — but one of my favourites is the one he used
to tell about his first homecoming for ten years or so.

His father was, I believe the vicar of Llanrhaeadr, near
Denbigh and he had not seen his parents for at least a decade.
He arrived by train and walked the last few miles home.
Walking up the valley, he could see his father coming to meet
him. The first greeting, after ten years was, 'Hurry up, Noel.
Your mother has put the kettle on!'

Noel was in excess of six feet tall and I recall his showing me
a photograph of himself in younger days — truly a very smart
gentleman. He was still playing good golf well past the age
of eighty and many an opponent received a shock when he beat
them with only about seven clubs in his golf bag.

My favourite story though, of Noel, dates back to 1981 when
having just recovered from a major heart attack, I went down
to the Golf Club — the first time for many months. Who should
I meet on the car park? — Noel. He came across the car park,
shook me by the hand and said, 'They tell me you haven't

111

been very well, Alf.' I said, 'I haven't but I'm feeling better now.' Then, he made a remark I will remember for the rest of my days, 'No. I did not know that you had been so ill, and nearly died. My God, I'd have hated to miss your funeral!'

Thank you, Noel for many happy hours of conversation when I was acting 'Pro.', helping Roy out in the professional shop in Oswestry. Knowing you was one of the happiest times of my life, but sadly Noel has 'gone to pastures new' — as we all must do one day — as has another great friend of mine, Norman O'Leary, the local milkman.

Many a story Norman could tell and as I sit here writing, my mind often wanders to those happy times. May you both Rest in Peace.

Noel and I were once in the Royal Shrewsbury Hospital at the same time, but in different wards and would send messages to each other via the nurses. One little message I received was that the Sister in charge of his ward asked him one morning, 'Have your bowels moved, Mr. Reece?' His reply was, 'Where to?'

Chapter 31

Shire Stallion

IT was a February morning. Jack Owen had not been too well. A village blacksmith like myself, now he worked for himself, but had previously been with Jim Pearce who ran the blacksmith shop after the death of his father at West Felton. Jack was working from the Smithy at Queens Head. 'Jack the Black' as he was often called, made arrangements for me to help him out one morning to shoe two of Mr. Suckley's shire horses from Brogyntyn — getting them ready for Peterborough Show in March.

At Mr. Suckley's farm there was an original old Smithy of yesteryear — complete with old hand bellows. Jack was well enough to come with me and blow the fire to get the shoes hot. It saved quite a bit of time to have someone who knew what he was doing. Although I was back into full-time shoeing, I had not shod a shire horse for many years. Much more physical strength is required than for shoeing a pony or a hunter. We arrived at John Suckley's who said to me, as I got out of my van, 'Which one do you want to do first? The quiet mare or the stallion who requires a bit more time as he gets restless?' It was the first I had heard that one of the horses was a bit 'rough' to shoe. However, it was no good moaning — shoeing had to be done and that's what we were there for. 'We'll have the rough one first,' I said.

As Mr. Suckley led this big black stallion down the yard towards the Smithy, my spirits dropped and I began to wonder what I had let myself in for. It looked a lot bigger than any shire horse I had ever shod. The first thing Jack did after we had got this massive shire into the Smithy was to drop a three-inch piece of piping which fitted into two big staples in place across the door about four feet off the ground. The heavy bar stretched right across the opening.

'What's that for?' I enquired.

'It's so we can get out and not this bugger!'

Two twitches were then produced; one was put on the horse's nose and one on his ear. Twitches are supposed to quieten a restless animal. Jack then gave me a pikel stale about four feet long with the remark, 'Give him two or three belts in his ribs.'

'What for?' I said.

'Well, to let him know you are here.'

I said, 'You can't hit a horse for nothing.'

'Alright, you'll see,' said Jack.

After a couple of minutes or so of struggling with the stallion, I gave him a couple of smacks which seemed to let him know I was there.

After about a quarter of an hour, I had all four feet cut down, ready for the shoes to be fitted (which Jack had heated).

After about another twenty minutes or so of struggling with this so called 'gentle giant', the shoes were ready to be nailed on. As I was sitting down for a 'breather' on my shoeing box before nailing the shoes on, the horse gave a big rear, nearly escaping from the hands of John Suckley and the waggoner. As it came down to earth, the waggoner looked up at the horse's nostrils and in a loud voice shouted at the horse, 'I'll bloody kill you.' I said, 'If you're going to do that, kill the bugger before I put these shoes on!' He did not kill the horse and eventually we did get a set of shoes on — after a lot more cursing and shouting.

The next horse, much better behaved, was soon shod and away we came for home. After travelling about five miles (nearly home) Jack said, 'Stop the van. We'll have to go back to Mr. Suckley's.'

'What for?' I asked.

His reply was, 'I've forgotten to tip the water out of the tub and if any birds fall into it, they'll drown.'

114

The blacksmith's shop at the farm was only used when horses were shod. I have often wondered whether anyone would ever believe an old village blacksmith was concerned enough about young birds falling into a water tub — but turn back we did and the water was emptied down the drain!

I was not Mr. Suckley's regular blacksmith, Jack Owen was. But as one did have the occasional few days off, we would ring each other and help out. I came in one summer evening at about nine o'clock, having been out shoeing all day from early morning and looking forward to a nice hot bath. As I arrived, Vera came out and said, 'Mr. Suckley has rung. He has lost a shoe and will you please ring him as Jack is away.' I phoned Mr. Suckley's home and he told me, 'We've lost a front shoe, Alf, but I've got the shoe. I wonder if you could possibly nail it on for me as I'm going to a show tomorrow.'

I also had a seven o'clock early start for shoeing next day, so I said, 'I'll be out with you at six o'clock tomorrow morning.'

'We're leaving for the show at five o'clock.'

There was no way I would be able to go next morning so there was nothing else for it but to go then. 'I'll be out in twenty minutes.'

Getting my weary old legs going, I arrived at Mr. Suckley's at about a quarter to ten that night. It did not take long to put one shoe on and as I finished, out came a bottle of beer. As I sat outside on my shoeing box talking to Mr. Suckley and drinking my pint, I thought what a great character he was. He would be seventy years old then, twenty years my senior and still working! What a wealth of stories he could tell and as we talked away, I did not feel half so tired and the beer made me feel better. Bidding him goodnight and with his thanks ringing in my ears, I thought why cannot all farmers and people be as nice as John Suckley.

My brother Jack and I were to go and shoe a horse for Mary Woolham. The horse, a three-year-old, had never been shod before. We arrived at her farm to be informed that she Mary, would hold the pony and feed it ginger-nut biscuits — to keep it quiet while we shod it. I smiled to myself and thought, 'That's a new trick!'

115

However, I tried to pick up the pony's foot only for him to shy away. Time and time again this happened. I said to Mary, 'We're not getting on very well. How many more biscuits have you?'

'Two in this packet, but I've another in the house.'

'Right,' I said, 'You go into the house and in about half an hour, bring out the coffee and the other packet of biscuits.' By this time, Charlie, her husband had arrived and persuaded Mary to do just that. He said, 'Leave the job to the professionals.' Before Mary had disappeared into the house, we had the twitch in the pony's nose and after a couple of sharp slaps on his belly, we soon started to make headway. The pony was shod in double-quick time and was standing quite placid as Mary appeared with the coffee and another packet of ginger nuts.

'How did you get him to stand so quiet?' she asked.

'By whispering in his ear what I would do if he didn't behave,' I said. When shoeing a horse, there can be only one boss — the blacksmith. If the horse is allowed to 'boss' you, you are not much good.

As I remember, it was a good cup of coffee and the•ginger nut biscuits very tasty. Whenever I see Mary on the golf course, I enquire if she still buys ginger nut biscuits — its become a little standing joke between us.

Chapter 32

Home for Unmarried Mothers

I HAVE never been involved much in the shoeing of racehorses — the odd point-to-point runner, but this incident does involve a racehorse.

A lady owner trainer in our area was on the phone one Saturday night to report her horse, which she was hoping to race the following Saturday, at Bangor on Dee was lame. Her call meant my turning out early the following morning, Sunday, to remove a shoe. I found a bit of gravel embedded in the sole of the foot, quite a common complaint, quickly attended to and no big problem.

With any amount of luck and plenty of attention, the horse would be able to race the following Saturday. Part of the treatment was for the shoe to be left off for a few days for the foot to be poulticed with hot dressings. This was my advice to the owner, as I asked her to ring me on Wednesday morning to let me know how the horse was getting on and whether he was ready to have his road shoe put back on.

Racehorses have to have plenty of roadwork before a race, and if fit enough to have his shoe put on, two days' roadwork would help that animal considerably. If not fit, he would have to be witdrawn, and if two days' notice were not given, then the race entrance fees would be lost. It was essential a decision be made on Wednesday on its fitness. I never answered the telephone; my wife, Vera, did so always. Too much time is lost answering the telephone when there is work to be done.

'How can I give Vera a complicated message regarding the horse's fitness?' the owner said.

'O.K.,' I said, 'You ring me dead on eight on Wednesday morning and I'll answer the phone personally and get the message direct.' I told Vera on Tuesday night I would answer the phone next morning at eight, to speak to the horse's owner, as promised.

Next morning, dead on eight, as the pips went on the radio, the phone rang. Thinking it was the lass owner of the lame horse, I thought 'I'll have a bit of fun,' and in a laid-back voice, I said, 'Good Morning, this is the home for unmarried mothers. Can I help you?'

There was a slight pause and then a voiec said,

'Oh, I wanted Alf Strange, the farrier.'

'Oh,' I said, 'he visits every afternoon.'

At that, the phone was put down at the other end as I did too. Before I had time to think who it was, the phone rang again and I answered properly this time. It was the owner of the lame horse who explained that the horse was better and could I put the shoe back on. This I agreed to do and with the words, 'I'll see you later this morning.' I put the phone down, only for it to promptly ring again. Again, I answered properly and it was the same lady who had rung dead on eight o'clock.

'Is that you, Alf?' she enquired.

'It is,' I said.

'Oh, good,' she said. 'I rang you earlier and got some damned unmarried mothers' home.'

— and then it dawned on me who it was, a titled lady who wanted her horse shoeing. I went to her stables many time never disclosing it was I who had said: 'This is the home for unmarried mothers.' I have an idea, though, she knew because of the many sideways glances she gave me when I was shoeing her horses. By the way the horse that had been lame came third in his race.

One of my favourite places to go shoeing was Sid Phillip's at Bradenheath. He had acquired an old horse just to hack around the lanes. Visits to Sid's were invariably in the evenings, for two reasons. One was that he would be at home to get the horse ready and the other that he made very good wine of various makes and strengths which, after we had shod the horse (and not before) he would try out on my brother Jack and myself.

'Fancy a drop of this? he would ask. If you don't like it, say so, because I think it needs perhaps another week or two to mature.' Many's the night, after a wine-tasting at Sid's, there would be no need to call in Ellesmere on the way home for a pint. Sid's horse, always quiet, would often nod off to sleep, dropping his head forward over the fence. Once, it had a shock, literally, for he had leaned too far forward, touching the electric fence with his nose. I wondered what had happened as the electric shock hit me as well. It took quite a while to quieten the old horse down, but I do not recall his ever going to sleep again. Not that it would have mattered had he done so, for after that the electric fence was always switched off. But he was not to know that.

Chapter 33

A Sunday Morning

A GOOD scrub down in the shower was always necessary but Saturday night was bath night. A soak in the bath with plenty of Radox salts helped to keep the old muscles from seizing up. I suppose it was a ritual from childhood days — Saturday night, bath night — with the old tin bath in front of the old black-leaded fire grate and a liberal supply of carbolic soap. However, many years ago, after a good old soak in a hot bath on Saturday night, I received a phone call from a young girl aged, I suppose, about nine — nearly in tears. 'Alf,' she said, 'Can you come and shoe my pony in the morning. Mummy should have rung you in the week but she forgot and I have been away for the week and just found that the pony has not been shod. I want to jump in a gymkhana tomorrow.' (tomorrow being Sunday)

I had one pony already booked to shoe on that Sunday morning at half past nine so it meant I would have to be at the young lass's place by eight o'clock — a distance of about ten miles.

'Please, Alf,' she said, 'I do really want to go to the gymkhana tomorrow.'

'Is your mother there?' I enquired.

'No, she has gone out with daddy and won't be in till late.'

'Right,' I said. 'I will be at your place before eight in the morning. Make sure the pony is in the stable. Leave a note on the table and by the clock, telling your mum I will be there before eight o'clock, as I have another pony to shoe later on.'

Little did I think as I went to bed how calamitous next morning was going to be.

Up early, I arrived at the first pony's place at about five to eight. Everywhere was locked up — and two (Rottweilers) loose in the yard. After talking to them quietly, I managed to get the gate open, keeping one eye on the dogs. I managed to get to the front door, ringing the bell for a full thirty seconds without response. There being no pony in the stable, I rang again and eventually the girl's mother appeared. As she opened the door, she said, 'My God, what do you want?'

I said, 'Just the pony in the stable.'

'Oh, God,' she said. 'I forgot to ring you.'

'Didn't you find any notes last night when you came in?' I asked.

'I was in no fit state to look for any notes. All I wanted to do was go to bed.'

As she adjusted the strap on the tight fitting nightie, she said, 'Come in for a cup of coffee.'

'No thanks,' I immediately replied.

'All I want is the pony so I can bang some shoes on and be away.'

She went to the bottom of the stairs and in a really raucous voice, called the daughter, 'The blacksmith's here to shoe your pony.' I could hear mumbling dissent from upstairs but eventually, two girls appeared, dressed in jeans followed by their mother in the tightest pair of pink coloured trousers, and pink jumper I had ever seen. Talk about 'letting it all hang out'. She also wore a pair of flip-flop slippers.

I knew I had to keep out of sight as this Thelwell type of pony did not like blacksmiths. I can see him now as the girls approached him to catch him and put the halter over his head. He was in a small paddock and I knew he was not going to be caught easily. He trotted away from them and then with a shout from one of the girls — 'Mother,' she shouted. A slightly open gate led into a fifteen acre field. Mother took off towards the gate but in her tight-fitting pink trousers, she was no match for the pony. She was losing a yard in every three. The pony won and was now in a fifteen-acre field — doing an extended trot, breaking wind with every other step.

'Well,' I said. 'It looks as if you've had it for the gymkhana today.'

Father appeared and, leaning on the gate, he shouted loudly, 'I'll catch that bugger one day — with me gun!'

The girls started to cry, mother with her tight-fitting everything started to tell father what she thought of him. We went back towards the stables when all of a sudden, the pony passed us. Why, I don't know. What made him come in is still a mystery to me. Perhaps he thought he had had his bit of fun for that day. He was caught and in no time at all, I put a set of shoes on and everyone was happy. I then accepted a cup of coffee.

At the next farm, the pony was already in the stable and in no time at all, a set of shoes were put on. Away for home leaving another satisfied customer. When working for oneself, if you give a decent service, you will always have plenty of work and in the Horse World, Saturday and Sunday are just ordinary days. On arriving home that Sunday morning, I suggested to Vera, 'Let's go to this gymkhana for a couple of hours or so,' which we did.

There with dad and mum was this little lass, all dressed up in her riding gear ready for her first event to jump about six small jumps. The pony was quite capable of doing just that — but not today! It ploughed through the jumps like a tank. Poles and rails were flying everywhere. We stayed to watch a few more events that the pony was in but it was his bad day. The pony had no intention of doing anything right — but I suppose, a good time was had by all. I suppose mum did not have to get dinner — a few butties and an apple would be sufficient for them that day — and I suppose dad could pop off for a pint and then a snooze in his car — that would suit him. So, a good day was had by all — Horse People live in another world.

122

Chapter 34

Donkey Drops

I TOOK a phone call one evening and a voice at the other end of the telephone enquired, 'Are you a farrier?'

'I am,' was my reply.

'Well,' he said, 'I am the General Manager of the Apollo Circus and we are giving a performance tonight in Oswestry on the car park. Will you come and trim our donkey's feet?' My reply was 'Yes, when?'

'Oh,' was his reply, 'in the morning.'

'No chance,' I said. 'I am booked up all day tomorrow.'

'We are desperate,' was his answer.

'I am coming Oswestry way in the morning early,' I said. 'If you will have the donkey ready, I will cut his feet on my way through.'

'What time will that be?'

'About seven o'clock,' I said.

'Fine,' was his reply. 'I'll see you at seven o'clock in the morning.'

Arriving a bit before seven o'clock, I found no sign of human life at all but there were two lovely coloured ponies tethered, well groomed and well shod. Some distance away was the donkey, eyeing me over. I went to him and was surprised to find his front feet were well trimmed but his back feet were very long and a real mess. There was still no sign of life from any of the caravans.

I put my hand on the donkey's back and started to run my hand down his rump when all hell broke loose. The donkey started to 'heehaw' lashing out with both hind legs at the same time and bucking like a bronco. After a short while, he went quiet and I tried again, with the same response.

At that I heard a laugh from one of the caravans — and then it dawned on me. This was the donkey no one could ride in the circus show. He had been trained to buck and kick when anything or anyone put weight on his back. So, I did not bother to put my hand on his back — I just picked his feet up by the hoof and in no time at all, I trimmed both his feet — to the surprise of the General Manager, who had by now, arrived on the scene — another lesson learnt, another memory to record. If my memory serves me correct, the price for trimming the donkey's feet would be about 75p — but don't forget that I, the village blacksmith, have done work for the General Manager of Apollo Circus. As I sit here writing, my mind goes back to those days. I wonder what happened to the Apollo Circus. Did they ever make it to television? Did the donkey ever achieve any sort of fame with the Bucking Bronco act? I wonder . . .

The lot of a village blacksmith is not always easy in dealings with some characters you meet along the way. In my early days as village blacksmith, I had the feeling certain people looked down on me, but as I have gone through my life, I have come to realise that I was as wise and my skill as a farrier was, in many cases, far superior to those of a lot of my customers.

I was, one morning, at stables trying to shoe a very difficult horse, that had not been handled properly. I had the feeling that some time in its life it had been ill treated as well. The more I tried to get its feet up, the more unruly he became. I told the new owner of the horse to try and handle the horse and work with him a bit more and that I would come again the next week to try and put a set of shoes on him. As I was about to leave, a rather loudmouthed horse dealer who, I think, owned the animal drove into the yard. He enquired whether the horse had been shod. 'No,' I said. 'He's not fit to shoe and I am no good to anybody with a broken leg.'

'Call yourself a blacksmith?' he said. 'When I took a horse that was a bit wild to so-and-so to be shod, he (the blacksmith) used to chuck him over and I would sit on his head and hold him down.'

'Good on you,' I said. 'You are just the man I'm looking for. Tell you what — if you'll sit on this bugger's head, I'll shoe him for nothing!'

There was a slight pause and then he remembered another appointment for which he was already late and he drove out of the gate. I said to the lady of the stables to try and fix up for him to come again within the next fortnight to sit on the horse's head but do you know? He couldn't find time!

Eventually we shod the horse, after he had quietened down a bit. Whenever I met that man in the future, he was always in a hurry — no time to talk — but I did have the pleasure of showing how brave he really was in front of a few other people. A true blacksmith is not afraid of any horse, provided there is someone to hold its head or if the horse is tied up.

While on the subject of rough and wild horses I remember a fairly local lad, Fred Walford from Criftins. His daughter, Sandra, had a quiet pony she used to deliver papers with and we used to shoe it. However, they had another, a younger one that had never been shod.

It befell Fred, her father, to bring him to the Smithy to have its first set of shoes on. I don't think Fred was much of a horseman and I don't think he was a lover of horses — I am sure so, after this particular Saturday morning. You always expect trouble at the first time of shoeing but I don't think Fred bargained for what happened in that hour or so.

Somehow or other, the horse fell three times and Fred fell down five times — I don't think the horse was very popular that morning and I don't think I figured very highly in his book of best friends. How he managed to fall down five times, I don't know.

Chapter 35

Flashing Lights

POLICE in patrol cars were starting even in our village with the loss of the local bobby — again another retrograde step for society.

One Sunday at about 5.30 a.m. there was banging on our front door. Half asleep, I opened the bedroom window and on the front at Brow Farm was a patrol car with its lights flashing and two irate policemen informing me all my cows were on the main road. That I told them I did not own any cows did not pacify them. They were up and they demanded I get up immediately. As I arrived on the front of Brow Farm, one officer was going to book me for allowing cattle to stray on the main road. I again told them at that time, I did not own any cows, only heifers and yearlings and then, of course, it dawned on me they did not know the difference between a cow and a heifer.

Being of townie descent, after giving me another lecture about the rights and wrongs of cattle straynig, I still protested they were possibly someone else's. All to no avail. I asked them where the cattle were.

'They have gone down Tetchill Lane.' (Tetchill Lane being a small lane leading off the main road to Tetchill — the small village about two miles away.

The policemen got into their 'flashy' patrol car and with a final word, warning me to get the cattle off the road. By this time, Vera, Alan and Valerie were up and dressed so off we went, down Tetchill Lane, to find the cattle had got into

126

another field through an open gate and as I thought, they were not mine.

I told this story a few weeks later to one of our local village bobbies and his reply to me was, 'If that had been me, I would have said "Come and give me a hand to get the cattle in", but because they were in a posh patrol car, you let them drive away.' He also said, 'I expect that Sunday morning, they had been having a snooze in a lay-by and had been woken to come to your place.'

Unfortunately, our farm is the only road-side farm in the five miles between Whittington and Ellesmere and we always seem to get the blame for any cattle straying. In telling this story, I am only trying to record the changes in village life that have taken place in my lifetime. Quoting Alistair Cooke in his 'Letters from America' — 'It has all happened in our lifetime.'

To end this little story, only a few months ago, I was reminiscing with our former policeman Peter Nicholas about things in general and he told me an amusing story of one incident in his police career. He had to regularly visit an old lady who kept, in days gone by, two maids. After a few drinks, she said she was having trouble with one of them. She said to the policeman, 'Next time you come, I want you to hold her while I thrash her.'

Chapter 36

Cold Comfort Farm

LITTLE did I think what was going to befall me in 1970. We had a good Christmas, and celebrated the New Year. Farming and blacksmithing were going well and we had been at Brow Farm for sixteen months. We were slowly 'getting on our feet' as the saying is, with a full time farm helper, Ian Mellor. This meant that we could have a break from the incessant grind of the milking — in fact, life was running so smoothly, we felt it was too good to be true.

In January that year, we had some hard frosts which froze Hardwicke Pool quite solid but our big field which borders Hardwicke Pool has plenty of shelter from the pool cover on one side and a small coppice on the other. At that time, there was a dilapidated shed in one corner of the field, which meant we were able to keep seven big heifers out. We had to break the ice every morning for them to drink. The first job after morning milking was to take the heifers some hay and break the ice on the pool.

Straight after breakfast, Ian had gone down to do this but in less than ten minutes, was back gasping that all seven heifers had fallen through the ice into about twelve feet of water. The ice was too thick for him to break with an old axe we kept for the job down by the pool. We grabbed a couple of fourteen pound sledge hammers and ran to the pool a — distance of about half a mile. Shouting as I went to Vera to ring for the Fire Brigade the sight which greeted my eyes was unbelievable. The seven heifers were swimming about in a hole about fourteen feet in diameter which swans, geese and coots kept open by swimming continuously in circles — stopping the ice from forming in that particular area.

They had gone across the thick ice to get a drink and one by one must have slipped in and were not able to get out, the ice being too thick for them to break.

Standing either side of the hole on the thick ice, Ian and I started to hit the ice with our sledge hammers, breaking a shallow trench towards the side of the pool, oblivious to the danger we were both in. After about ten minutes, we had a channel about two feet wide. By now, we were totally exhausted but could hear the welcome sound of the fire engine arriving at the entrance to the field — Joe Butler in charge.

But we could not persuade any of the heifers to come up the channel to safety Ian and I had cut out for them and by now, they were showing signs of distress.

Stuart Deakin suggested two of them take a ladder to go to the far side of the hole. Holding each end of the ladder, they slowly managed to push the heifers to the channel and safety. As the first heifer went up the channel, five more followed. But as soon as the first heifer's feet touched solid ground, she stopped still, leaving the others in deep water.

This is when manpower came in — we literally dragged the leading heifer to dry land and used the same procedure with the other five. Sadly, the seventh heifer succumbed to the intense cold. Nothing more could be done for her so we concentrated on the six live heifers, all lying exhausted on the field. Ian fetched a tractor and trailer from the farm and Vera, as only a wife would think, sent a flask of coffee, a bottle of Scotch and a bottle of Stones' Ginger Wine. Only then did we realise how cold and wet we all were. I think, it was one of the coldest days of the winter.

After a couple of hours and two empty bottles and — by now, the assistance of George Wyse, the vet who gave the heifers injections (and helped with the bottles, as well!), the six surviving heifers were bedded down and their survival assured.

We came back to the house to warm by a roaring fire, a cup of coffee each (no more alcohol) and the realisation that by now, it was three o'clock.

Wishing to show my gratitude to the five firemen involved in the rescue of my heifers (by today's value, something like £7,000) I offered Joe some money to buy a drink. He refused stating that firemen were not allowed to accept.

However, I did deposit a few pounds over the bar at the Railway Hotel with Mrs. Thomas which meant they had a few free pints when they paid their visits to the pub after training on Tuesday evenings.

It does not sound much by today's values but £5 was a lot of money in those days — indeed, to me it was. Without the assistance of Ellesmere Fire Brigade, I would have lost a lot of money. One of them, Stuart Deakin, went up to his armpits in the ice cold water.

I am told money is irrelevant but the loss, at that stage of my life, would have surely 'rocked the boat'. So I say Thank You to the Ellesmere Fire Brigade for their help in saving my heifers. You acted over and above your call of duty on what we've agreed when we've met over the years, was indeed one of the coldest days we ever experienced and without the Whiskey Macs and hot coffee, we might not have been able to carry out the rescue. Today, proudly displayed in the Fire Station at Ellesmere is a photograph of the Ellesmere Division of Fire Men receiving an award for their outstanding bravery on that cold January day in 1970.

Chapter 37

Holy Pig Meal!

HINSTOCK is a village about 30 miles east of Welsh Frankton — not far in a modern motor car. The incident I am about to recall happened on a Saturday morning when I fetched a bag of pig meal from North Shropshire Farmers in Cross Street, Ellesmere. Somehow that bag landed in Hinstock.

I loaded the pigmeal on the back carrier of my Morris 8 to take it home to the Brow. Back home, to my dismay, there was no pigmeal on the carrier — it must have dropped off somewhere between Ellesmere and Frankton. We searched, but no luck. Panic stations — there was no chance of getting another on Saturday afternoon! North Shropshire Farmers was shut.

I went to the police station to see if anyone had reported a dropped bag of pigmeal but no luck. Harry Speke, the sergeant said, 'Someone may have picked it up and will report their find later in the day. If so I'll give you a ring.'

In those days the police would give you a ring; today you would more likely get a summons for an insecure load. That night, the pigs had to have a mixture of dairy nuts, chicken meal, a bit of bran, beet pulp and a few household scraps all mixed up together.

Harry Speke rang later that evening, 'Your bag of pig meal has been found and I'm pleased to tell you it's at the Vicarage at Hinstock.' It appears the vicar of Hinstock had been travelling towards Frankton on the Ellesmere Road and had taken it home to Hinstock with him. Why he had not dropped it off at the Police Station in Ellesmere, I do not know. Perhaps he thought, if nobody claimed it, he could raffle it off at the church Garden Fete later in the year! However, that was that. A journey to Hinstock it had to be — no way could I afford to lose a bag of pig meal. Valerie, Alan and Vera enjoyed a round trip of sixty miles and there was a special treat on the way home — chips from up the hill — Sall's specials. I can't remember whether I put anything in the church box. I suppose the bag of pig meal worked out quite dear enough.

Talking of Morris 8's reminds me of a job a village blacksmith had to do often in those days — making a new main leaf for the springs of that car, fitting two new brass brushes and re-setting the springs. This would bring one side of the car up quite a bit — possibly a foot or more — which meant the other three springs had to be given the same treatment to bring the car up level all round.

It was a time-consuming job because one could only get the leaves off the springs at a certain temperature — a trick my dad taught me — no books required! If the spring had been tempered too hard, it would snap again — if too soft, it would sag or straighten out and would have to be done again. Main leaves and new leaves were made out of the old redundant carts and wagons. A 'cherry red' heat was about right, my dad used to say, 'If you get the spring any hotter, then put it down and let it cool naturally, and then start again.' I don't know how many car springs I replaced without going through my day book, possibly a few hundred. I remember the pride of making one new main leaf and resetting the spring for G. Cleveley's Garage at Criftins and the price was seven shillings and six pence. How do I know that? Well, it appears that Bernard, my accountant had somehow or other written in my day book in his handwriting, in pen, this, 'Price One New Main Leaf for Morris Eight and Resetting Same 7/6'. That price and writing stands out for all to see now in my old day book of the late forties.

Most of the lads in the area had by then, Morris 8 or Ford 8 cars. Gone were the days of going to work on a bike into Ellesmere or to local farms. The lads of the village were on the move to Smiths of Whitchurch, fourteen miles away —

Marchweil Trading Estate, the same distance — Sankeys at Wellington, thirty miles one way — progress!

The price of the average Morris or Ford was within their financial capabilities — which brings me to resetting some of these springs — a job that could only be done on a Saturday afternoon as the majority of car owners worked until Saturday at one o'clock.

I would then be able to have their car, take one of the front springs off, strip it down, reset the leaves, then let them go cold, whilst I did something else, like welding a couple of cracks in the mudguards. By the time you had done that and put the spring back on the car, time to 'knock off'. Yes, the village blacksmith was expected to work on a Saturday afternoon — and did!

As stated, this would have left one front side of the car up about a foot. No problem, the owner would go to work all week like that, then on the following Saturday afternoon, have the other spring done — The same routine — go to work all week with the complete front end up, then the following week, one back spring would receive the same treatment. Eventually, by the following Saturday night, the car would look level all round. For a payment of I think, about two pounds for the work done, another satisfied car driver would be found. What chance today of going from Welsh Frankton to Sankeys? — scarcely able to see over the bonnet of your car — so many millimetres of tread on your tyres. What was 'tread' on a rubber wheel? I am sure some of the lads thought a smooth tyre gave a smoother ride!

Chapter 38

Polished Salesman

ONE arrival in the village one day : a taxi from Oswestry — driver complete with peaked cap. Sitting in the passenger seat, dressed immaculately, another gentleman, who when he got out of the taxi, had in his hand a gallon can of car cleaner — or so he said.

It was on special offer, bankrupt stock and if my memory serves me right, priced at about £1 10 shillings.

He carried with him a piece of cloth and he then tipped some of the so called 'car cleaner' on the one mudguard of my old Austin 12. He gave it a good polish and it came up like new — a very impressive demonstration.

I decided to buy the 'car cleaner' in the taxi, which carried, at a rough guess, about one hundred identical cans. I told the salesman, 'You will have to take a cheque.' He seemed reluctant but eventually, did so and away he went. In our area that day, I believe he sold all his 100 cans — by giving the same demonstration — a drop on a bit of cloth — a good rub — and a sale was made. However, I think it was Eric Jones, Ron's Dad, who rang me that evening and enquired whether I had bought any of the car cleaner.

'Have you tried it ?' he said.

'No, but I will tomorrow.'

Then he said, 'Ive tried to clean my car with it. I think it's only diesel or paraffin mixed with a drop of oil — nothing like the stuff he used in his demonstration — out of a different tin altogether. How did you pay him ?' he asked. 'Oh, by

134

cheque,' was my reply, 'but he seemed reluctant to take one. Cash and pound notes were his main concern.'

At that time, I don't suppose he expected a village blacksmith would have the sense to stop a cheque. Next morning, I rang the bank to stop the cheque.

Imagine the shock this 'spiv' type of character received a few days later for he had used my cheque as part payment for bed and breakfast at the Lion Hotel, Shrewsbury — none of your ordinary bed and breakfast for this bloke — star treatment he required. A couple of days later, the phone rang and a voice at the other end said, 'Are you Alf Strange, the blacksmith?'

'I am,' was my reply.

'What do you mean by stopping your cheque?'

'Well,' I said, 'You conned the whole area with your so called Car Cleaner. It serves you right to be embarrassed cashing my cheque at the Lion in Shrewsbury.'

His reply was, 'I'll be with you in half an hour to sort you out.'

'I'm not going anywhere,' was my reply.

That was over 45 years ago and I am still waiting for his arrival. I think that was the village's first 'brush' with a 'spiv' — a new word after the 1939-45 war used for shady characters. Where he came from no one ever found out — a mystery man from the smoke — 'townie' type of character.

Chapter 39

Vera's Birthday Present

AFTER a great deal of saving, and selling the odd dozen eggs at the door (unbeknown so to Bernard, our accountant, a pound note from her mother and so on, Vera had the princely sum of £5 which she blew on a sitting room chair from Astons.

When I went with Sid Jones to collect it from Oswestry, there was snow on the ground, and it had just started to snow again. After a struggle we managed to get the chair into the back of the Austin 12.

Little did I think as we set off for home what an eventful journey we would have. The level crossing gates at Whittington were shut, and while waiting for them to open, glancing in the mirror, I realised the car behind was not going to stop. He rammed into the back of my car pushing me into the gates, which thank God, held, just as the train went thundering through. Had I not been there, I doubt whether the gates would have held the impact of his car, as ours had had a cushion effect.

In the front of his car was his wife, with a baby in her arms and there were two other children in the back — all five could have been under the train. All was well, however, except for the back-end of my car and the front of his. Vera's chair was still OK — what it would have been like had it been in the boot, I can only guess. The other driver admitted full liability, which, of course, it was.

In a day or two an insurance assessor came to look at the damage to my car which I suppose was worth about £120. I settled for his figure of £80. I did not mind running a car with the boot bashed in and I was able to do a reasonable repair myself to the boot. The cheque came a few weeks later, one Wednesday morning, market day in Oswestry.

A quick 'Directors' Meeting' with Vera and the decision was taken to buy another cow with the money we had received for the damage to the car. As luck would have it, the cow I bought proved to be a failure. She did not give much milk and eventually was sold a few months later for about half the money I paid for her six months earlier. My ill-gotten gains did not do me any good. But the chair lasted for many years and Vera had many pleasant hours watching our nine inch black and white television. As I remember, the driver of the car that ran into the back of me was an optician. His driving that day was no recommendation for his glasses.

Chapter 40

Bull in Water Tank

ONE of the most unusual jobs I ever had to deal with was a bull that had managed somehow or other, to get into a water tank holding I suppose two thousand gallons. It was used at the end of the cow house to catch rain water. Why I, the village blacksmith was called, was because the tap was broken and the water could not be let out. I was unable to get it free with a spanner but the old bull seemed quite contented, up to his neck in water.

The only thing I could think of was to fetch my oxyacetylene welder, cut a fairly large hole in the tank to let the water out and then to weld a plate back in place and hopefully, all would be well. This we did but the old bull would not jump and no amount of slapping, shouting, or other form of persuasion worked — the bull refused to move.

Well, I thought, 'I might as well weld the plate back in place while I am here to save another journey.' I had just started when all of a sudden, the bull roared, stood on his hind legs clearing the edge of the tank with feet to spare and galloped like hell down the road with his tail in the air — followed by the farmer and two or three men.

After a fair old chase, he was recaptured and brought back but as he came into the yard, he gave the water tank a wide berth.

The only thing I can think is that a spark from the welder must have landed on the bull's rear end and the shock must have made him jump out of the tank. So ends another little story and the answer to the question of how to get a bull out of a water tank!

We came to Brow Farm from the Perthy, in 1965, a distance of about two hundred yards. Life was very hectic, what with moving and trying to do a full day's blacksmithing as well — twenty-five hours in the day would not have been enough!

One little incident made me a believer in Fate. About two days before Christmas. Vera, as usual, up to her neck with moving house, was trying to put a bit into the Christmas celebration.

'Can you go and get a Christmas tree from the wood?' she said one day.

'I'll do my best,' was my reply.

We never bought a Christmas tree —always got one out of the wood and an artificial tree was unknown in those days? As I have stated, we live on a hill, and a very fast stretch of the main road passes us. I had just got my saw ready to get a tree, waiting to cross the main road, when over the top of the Brow Bank at high speed, came a lorry loaded with Christmas trees, and a tree — a real beauty — fell off the back of a lorry, literally 'at my feet'.

Taking it in to Vera, she said, 'You've not been long.' 'Well,' I said, 'You won't believe me but this tree fell off the back of a lorry.' I have had many a smile since when the saying 'It fell off the back of a lorry!' crops up.

Chapter 41

A Fair Cop at Hoylake

DUNCAN JONES, Jack and Norman Birch and I went to watch the Open golf at Hoylake on a day off in 1967. Hoylake Golf Club car park was nowhere near big enough so we had to park about two miles away taking a shuttle bus to the course.

Golf was really taking off as a spectator sport and booming as a pastime, now within reach of most people's pockets. We had a good day, but all good days have to come to an end. Thousands of people were trying to get off the course which borders a main road, along which traffic was travelling in both directions. This was being periodically held up by a policewoman on point duty in the middle of the road. Waiting for the signal to cross, I realised that she was my niece, Sheila. Quickly, I thought I'd have a bit of fun with Duncan when we get the signal to cross. I told him, 'I'm going to put my arm round that policewoman and give her a big hug.'

His face paled slightly, 'You'll get locked up if you do!'

'You watch me,' I replied.

The traffic stopped, and we started to cross. I paused by Sheila, put my arm around her and asked, 'How are you, Sheila? And how's your mum and dad?'

She was quite startled until she realised who I was. 'We're all fine,' she said. I then went on my way.

I could see a couple of tall policemen on the other pavement, and not wanting to get tangled up in any argument with them, I took off after Duncan, who by this time was a couple of

140

hundred yards ahead. He had only paused for a second to watch me talking to Sheila. Catching up, I said, 'It's my favourite pastime, chatting up pretty policewomen.' 'You'll do it once too often!' was his reply.

Only over a drink on the way home did I reveal she was my niece.

Chapter 42

Absent Friends

ON the Wednesday before Christmas 1946 my brother, Bill who had come out of the Royal Corps of Signals met up with a Harry Hughes. They both worked in Oswestry Post Office at that time. Having a drink in the pub called The Stone House, they made a vow to meet every Wednesday before Christmas at lunch time for a drink. The following year, 1947, I joined them. The following year my brother Jack and Doug Gough made the party up to five. Over the years, the company grew and is now twenty strong. We gather every year at the Old Boote Hotel in Whittington.

Each year a toast master is proposed by the senior members and he is not informed until the evening of the dinner and then it is left entirely to him to organise the venue and programme for the following year.

In about 1975, a special tie was made with the motif of a foaming jug of beer with the letters 'A.F. — Absent Friends'. Only eighteen were made and the rule is that if a member passes away, the tie is handed back to the club. We still have sixteen of the original ties left, though many of our friends have passed to pastures new over the years — some quite young — which brings it home to those of us left how uncertain life is.

At our gathering every year which is now held on the Wednesday before the Wednesday before Christmas, we all have to propose a toast but the first toast is always to 'absent friends', with a few seconds of silence to remember those who have gone before. 'Absent Friends' is now in its 47th year and in many cases, our sons are in the gathering. I have attended all 46 gatherings. I nearly missed a couple of times but was always able to make it. Thanks to the advancement of modern science, our little organisation I am sure will continue for many more years — I know, like me, the others always pencil in their new diaries the Wednesday before the Wednesday before Christmas — always the first entry to go in. This little gathering is so typical of the country scene. It is strictly non political, non religious (if any brings up either subject, a fine is to be paid into the kitty for a local charity). May this little gathering of ours continue — without them England would not be the same.

Chapter 43

Confessions of a Golf Addict

MY brother Jack, Phil Morgan, Ernie Just and I went by road to the FA Cup Final between Wolves and Blackburn in May 1960 — thirty three years ago. That match was to affect my life dramatically. As I remember, it was not a very good game. I think some critics described it as 'boring'. Wolves won 3-1. It was a very hot day and we left our car at Uxbridge and went by rail to Wembley.

The best part of the day was our visit before the game to Trafalgar Square, up the Mall, down past Buckingham Palace and Horse Guards Parade. It was, I think, the day after Princess Margaret and Lord Snowdon were married and there were beautiful decorations everywhere — a show that— only London can put on. On our way home, we called for a drink at a pub not far from Gailey — remember pubs shut at ten o'clock.

I remember saying to Phil, 'Well, if that's professional football and the amount of money players are getting for playing, I'm going to take up golf and not bother to watch professional football!' a resolution I stuck to for many a year.

We at Welsh Frankton had a good contact for tickets at Wolverhampton — Sam Lomas, an official of British Waterways. He used to get us tickets for the majority of evening games in the fifties against foreign teams — Spartac . . . . . Moscow Dynamos and it was he who got us the tickets for the Cup Final of 1960. We used to leave our car quite safely in Bright Street or Paget Street, not far from Molineux and

144

over the many years we left our cars there, no damage whatsoever was done to them. What chance today I wonder?

I had, by now, acquired my first set of clubs, off my brother Frank — £7 10 shillings — bag included and a few golf balls — not many though.

I rigged up an old type of net made out of scrap piping and some old beet pulp bags at the back of my Smithy. I only had to pop out for a few swings in between jobs — getting what we call today a 'grooved' swing.

For the first twelve months, I never went to a golf course — only to the net, or down our own fields when there was not much grass on them. Sometimes John Elder would come with a welding job and would have a few knocks in my net, or down the field.

When I went to his place I would take my clubs and drive towards the trough in his top meadow, 'practising' slices, hooks, shanks and often missing the ball all together. We treated the game as it should be treated, with a laugh and as a bit of fun.

Then to my first game on a golf course — 6.30 was the appointed time at Shrewsbury Golf Course one Sunday morning with my brother Frank, who by now, had a good golf handicap of 24 — Quite a Star! Jimmy Walker was the professional at the Old Shrewsbury Golf Club at Meole Brace.

There was no one about when we arrived so my brother Frank suggested we started at the fourteenth hole. Now, older members of golf clubs in Shropshire will remember the old fourteenth at Shrewsbury. What a hole to play your first real golf shot on! Out of bounds and rubbish, long grass etc., all to the left of the tee. My brother, Frank to go first — not a hole to have a vicious hook on — he did. No point in trying to find that ball! Me next. 'Keep to the right,' said Frank. I tried but took a similar line to his but not so far but in every bit as much trouble. My best ball lost with my first strike on a golf course and still only half past six in the morning! Frank played another ball, which, this time, he did not lose and then it was my turn again. I tried to remember what few good shots I had hit down the fields — don't swing too quickly — keep your head down, etc. — but to no avail.

145

The rough was waiting for my second ball as well, leaving me with only one more in my bag.

I decided to walk about 150 yards up the fairway away from all trouble and to my great surprise, hit that ball quite well. In the rough quite often from then onwards, I managed to find a ball or two, to keep me going for the rest of the round.

How many rules I broke that day — probably all — but the seed was sown and the 'Golf Bug' had captured another humble soul.

I am sure that in my case, work was less of a burden, because of golf. The odd game makes life more enjoyable and, as I see it, if you play badly, you can't wait to get another game quick enough to see if you can play better and if you play well, you can't get another game quick enough to see why you played better. Of all the games I have played, I think golf is the greatest leveller but also a character builder. You only have yourself to blame — unless you are playing mixed foursome — but that is a different game altogether — a subject I will not dwell on for many reasons!

After about another two months of practice down the field and by now, a member of Oswestry Golf Club (having paid the sub. of around £8 for the year), came the moment of truth, your first medal with a handicap of 24 and Arthur Jones as my marker — I then realised the difference a medal card in your hand, makes to your approach to the game and shots. After shots were thrown away here and there and everywhere in sand bunkers you did not know were there — but on regardless.

The only thing was my consistency — out in 50 for the first nine, back in 51 for the back nine — a gross of 101, less 24 — 77 net, but a lot learned — but, oh, so much more to learn before you get your own handicap down.

Holidays at a caravan at Rhyl took on a new meaning — join Abergele Golf Club (a weekly ticket about 7s.6d.); meet Frank at Hawkstone Park Golf Course after five o'clock at night. A round of golf then, in the early sixties, cost 2s.6d., half a crown golf balls, the best eight for a pound and little did I think that the young son of Alex and Agnes Lyle by the name of Sandy, would become one of the top golfers in the world. Many is the game of golf with and against Sandy I have played and also Ian Woosnam, affectionately known as 'Young Woosie' — but more of them later.

Having played football and cricket at a reasonable level locally, the game of golf offered a different and new challenge for me. Not being able to consistently hit a stationary ball was so frustrating. Various books were read — written by the 'greats' of the game — Henry Cotton, Tommy Armour to name but two but to no avail — and then the major decision was taken to go and have a lesson from John Powell, Wrexham's Golf Professional and an evening visit (too busy to go during the day) was arranged. After a few practice swings and then hitting a few golf balls, he said to me, 'Your golf clubs are far too whippy. You need stiffer shafts.' With being a blacksmith, arms and hands more used to swinging 14lb sledge hammers my need was for heavier clubs with stiff shafts. Of course, he had a good second-hand set for sale. How much, I can't remember I suppose about £1.50 each.

However, golf to me, as to many other addicts (ninety per cent comes to my mind) meant a decent set of clubs, not forgetting a better bag, new golf balls, — no excuses now. Birthdays took on a new meaning. Golf balls instead of handkerchiefs and ties and socks.

Many games were played with John Powell and one game of golf I remember was the day Doug Humphreys and I played with Jimmy McAlpine and John Powell in about 1970. Doug had, that year, played international golf for Wales — and here was I, a village blacksmith playing with the owner of one of the biggest construction companies in the country!

I can't think of any other game where one is accepted for for what you are, rather than who you are and golf today is well within the reach of most people, at the cost of a few fags and a pint or two less each week. But I sometimes wonder what my dad's farmer customers would have said. I suppose they would have wanted a few more bob knocking off their bills.

New friends were now being made as golf had taken over

completely from watching football — a day of playing golf instead. I am one of those lucky enough to have played a lot of championship courses for a few pounds for the day, Wentworth, Birkdale, Hoylake to name but a few and an annual day out with Duncan, brother Jack and Arthur in May was a regular event for many a year.

Duncan Jones had, by now, moved with his job as a salesman for Fullwood's up into Lancashire so we used to travel up there in May, and meet him. Duncan was not a regular player but a useful 18 handicapper — a very quick player — no practice swing — 'put the ball on the tee and hit it,' that was his theory (or 'miss it quick').

One of the most amusing incidents I have seen was at Lytham St. Annes no less. As most golfers know, Lytham is a Championship course with a long par three to start your round. With Duncan first on the tee to start our day's golf, I think he elected to use his driver. As he was about to hit his ball, he stopped. He had noticed to the right of the tee at an angle of about 45 degrees some caddies in their caddy shed. Duncan said to them, 'I wouldn't stand there if I were you.' The remark brought a loud laugh from the caddies and also from Jack and myself and Arthur — even Duncan can't hit a ball literally at right-angles! — but he did and the ball rattled around the shed, to the dismay and alarm of the caddies. They scattered in all directions and Duncan's remark was, 'I did warn them.' How he kept a straight face, I'll never know.

We had a great 36 holes of golf even after such an eventful start to the day, Duncan Jones is a terrific character. He had the ability to take charge of any situation. Many times, some of our evening meals have been hilarious, with Duncan 'pulling the waiter or waitress's leg.' Thanks Duncan, for many happy memories of my early days of golf.

Chapter 44

Lost Ball — Snow

DICK HUGHES, David James, Mike Elder and yours truly were playing a match one Saturday afternoon in the winter — three professional men; Dick Hughes, a lawyer, David James, a bank manager and Mike Elder, a doctor — and the village blacksmith! Snow was in the air when we drove off the first tee and personally, I thought there was not much sense in starting — not then knowing 'the will to win' of a half a crown by the other three. By the time we arrived at the seventh at Oswestry, there was possibly a good inch of snow on the green. I thought that surely we would be back in the Club House close by for a welcome drink and a warm soon — but no, down the eighth we went.

The snow was now coming quite thick and heavy and finding your ball on the fairway was becoming difficult. Surely we would go in after the ninth — but no, down the tenth away from the Club House we went, then the eleventh. By now, a freshening wind, made golf more difficult. Dick and I were, at this time, one up. Dick said to me on the eleventh green, 'Don't suggest going in because the match will be called a draw.' 'So what?' I thought.

On to the twelfth tee we went and down the thirteenth, the furthest green from the Club House. David and I both lost our golf balls on the thirteenth in, by now, the best part of two inches of snow — leaving the doctor and the lawyer to 'fight it out' — Dick I believe, eventually holing out for about eight, the doctor on for about five but still about sixteen feet from

the hole. I dared not suggest giving the doctor a win. Dick
would never have forgiven me.

After what seemed a hell of a long while and a lot of snow
cleared away, the doctor proceeded to putt, leaving himself with
about a one foot putt to win the hole — still silence from Dick
— but the doctor stroked the putt in to win the hole. It was
all square now. With honour restored, the doctor and Dick
shook hands and decided to walk in. By then, David and I
were well on our way to the Club House'.

What a way, I thought, 'to spend a Saturday afternoon!'

That is the way golf gets you and I suppose in their warm
office and surgery the following week, they would remember
every shot they played the previous Saturday.

Another incident on a golf course was the day we had out
at Little Aston, a top golf course in the Midlands. John Elder,
Dick Hughes, Dr. Mike Elder and again, me. It was the day
Harold Wilson, the Prime Minister was going to make an
announcement on the one o'clock news on whether he was going
to put a freeze on doctors' pay — so, our morning round of
golf had to be finished before one so that we could be in the
car to listen to the radio. We were quietly eating our sandwiches
when the announcement came that the pay freeze was not to
be implemented and the full eight per cent rise was to be
allowed. A cheer went up from the doctor who, by now, had
finished his butties and could not get out on the course quick
enough to try to add another 2/6d. to his rise.

This day was also one when I was not playing very well
and on one of the tees at Little Aston, the main railway line
runs along the back. Working on the line was a gang of railway
men, possibly a dozen or so. I played my tee shot ten yards or
so, barely reaching the end of the tee. My second was not much
better, neither was my third. All the time, I was being watched
by the gang of railway workers. As I was about to play my
fourth shot towards the green, one of the railway men shouted,
'Give him a b . . . . . hammer!'

I looked back but the embankment was steep and all covered
in brambles. I sure would have liked to have shown them that
I could use a hammer probably as well as them — maybe

better — I would have liked to see the look on their faces. Little did they realise that a village blacksmith did take a day off occasionally to have his game of golf!

On another occasion, after a day out playing golf, we four decided on the way home to have a meal at a hotel in Shrewsbury. We sat down at our table and the waiter came along. I think he was Italian. After taking our order for our meal, we ordered a round of drinks which seemed a long time coming. At the next table, were a young man, his girl friend and an older lady, which I assumed was the girl's mother. I think the young man was trying to impress his possible future mother-in-law. He had ordered a meal served 'flambe' . . . the type cooked and set fire to by the side of the table. This was being prepared by another Italian waiter who I don't think spoke much English and I am sure he did not understand the language. However, their meal was a disaster — they did not eat any of it and were leaving the table, refusing to pay. By this time, our drinks had arrived with another Italian waiter. John took one sip of his Scotch and then said, 'I ordered a Scotch and lemonade and this is Scotch and water. Go and change it.' This added to the confusion and panic surrounding our table. Other people were craning their necks and looking towards us. The Head Waiter came to try and sort out the problem of the meal on the next table but John thought his wrong drink of Scotch and water was every bit as important and said so a time or two. The climax of the whole incident was when both waiters tried to come through the swing door — one coming out and the other going into the kitchen — at the same time!

Eventually, order was restored. The young man did not have to pay, John had his Scotch and lemonade and as I remember, we had a good meal — another incident in the life of a village blacksmith recorded for future generations.

By now, a week of watching the golf at Fulford in Yorkshire was our holiday — a 'must' for something like twenty years — staying bed and breakfast at John and Lillian Parker's (The Windmill at Dunnington on the Hull Road, out of York itself). Many are the stories I could tell. It was, as I remember a very friendly tournament. You could talk and mingle with the players and share in the joy or sadness when watching lesser known players trying to qualify at nearby Strensal a — couple of days before. There would be possibly about a hundred younger golfers trying for about ten spots and then the tension of a 'sudden death' down the first for another dozen or so that were on the same score for another couple of places (or maybe only one) and the look on their dad's face when their son failed to qualify said it all.

I know because I have been a dad who did a fair bit of caddying and in my opinion, golf is not about the good shots you hit, it is more about forgetting the bad shots — a lot easier said than done. Talking to many professional golfers, the majority will say that one of the hardest rounds to play is the qualifying round for big tournaments, where perhaps you only have to shoot four par rounds to win a substantial sum of money. I am not trying to write a golfing book, just recording a few memories of my own golfing experiences. On one visit to the Benson and Hedges at Fulford in Yorkshire, I remember a terrific downpour, the heavens opened and in no time at all, the majority of the greens were submerged in inches of water. Play was suspended and the professionals were told to mark the places of their golf balls and retire to shelter. After about an hour or so, the sun broke through and the storm had passed by, leaving the green staff and any helpers they could rally, to clear the greens of water.

I was at the back of the third green, a short hole, par three, when a rake was thrust into my hand and a voice said to me, 'You look as if you can use a rake. Place it upside down and start to brush the water to the side of the green.' With a couple of other fellows, we did just that and I suppose in about half an hour the green was nearly playable.

I remember picking up a marker out of the water which I replaced, after I had swept the water. Then there came an announcement over the loudspeaker that play would commence at a certain time in about twenty minutes or so. By this time, Brian Hugget and another professional of Egyptian nationality, had appeared on the green. It was Brian Hugget's marker I had replaced.

The Egyptian pro was just through the green with his marker — but there was another marker on the green, nearer the hole which belonged to John O'Leary, the Irish golfer I found out from Brian Hugget who also enquired from me whether it was a quick-drying course. 'Oh, yes,' I said, 'It won't be long before you're playing again.' He moved away to talk to the other pro and I never did have the chance to tell him that I was on holiday from Shropshire, about 150 miles away.

A short while later, an announcement was made that play would commence in five minutes and all competitors were to be prepared to start again. Still no sign of John O'Leary and then a gesture which shows the loyalty to others in some people. Brian Hugget said to the Egyptian, 'You play your ball first, as you are the furthest away and if you want to play out and finish the hole, do so. I will then play my ball and play out the hole.' John O'Leary was, by this time, seen coming quite quickly about a couple of hundred yards away. He obviously had not anticipated play starting so soon. He arrived just in time to prepare to play his ball. Had Brian Hugget and the other pro not done what they did, John O'Leary would have been penalised for not being ready to start at his appointed time. I thought what a lovely gesture that was from one fellow pro to another.

No rules broken by any of the three players — just a little professional etiquette from one to another. Wouldn't it be nice if more gestures like that were more common in all sports, without so many petty arguments and squabbles, as seems to be the case today? I suppose today, with so much money at stake, one can become a wealthy man overnight by winning a single tournament — be it football, cricket, darts, etc. — some can command thousands of pounds for adding their names to some sports equipment or opening some shop or other — where will it end? Are they as happy as the average fellow who, maybe, works all his life and ends up owning his little terraced house? I sometimes wonder.

153

Chapter 45

Golfing Farmer

BY this time, with a lot of practice down the big field of ours, I had attained a handicap of four which to non-golfers who may read this, means that you can only drop four shots in a medal round to play to your handicap and as standard scratch on the majority of courses is 69, this means you have to take 73 shots or less to play to par. A single figure handicap opens the door to different types of competition and to retain your handicap means a lot of practice shots must be hit as often as possible and at this stage, I am proud to say I retained a handicap of between four and six for about fifteen years, until 1980 — a year I will never forget — but that will be written about in another book entitled *From Blacksmith to Brief Case* I think.

By now, my son, Alan, who had been playing golf for many years, had played for Wales at junior and youth levels and for Shropshire and Herefordshire at county level. I had never been chosen for county, although I had frequently come in the top fifteen in county trials, which, I personally think, were a waste of time as some players who scored badly in trials, still retained their places in the team. This, is my opinion, and mine alone. (You may think I have a 'chip on my shoulder' but I am only stating the facts as I saw them at the time). What was the point of playing a couple of rounds in the low seventies and when the county team was chosen, people who had scored in the mid eighties were chosen before you. However, I put my name on the Hargrove Shield a couple of times for Oswestry Golf Club — a shield played for annually by the top six players of all the golf courses in the two counties. I nearly had a famous victory once in a county match against Warwickshire. I was there to caddie for my son, Alan, in this match. Arriving at Ellesmere to meet the other players, one of the county players failed to turn up on the car park at 7.30 a.m. I rushed home for my clubs just in case the county team was one short. Arriving much later at Maxitowe Park in the midlands than the rest of the team, I was informed that I would be playing. Having just driven about a one hundred mile journey. Quite quickly, I played in the morning foursomes with Geoff Roberts and if my memory serves me right, we had a good game and lost by the respectable score of two and one.

After a quick lunch, the moment of truth — on your own, on the first tee — nobody to blame, only yourself! I was to play a fellow who I believe, a couple of years earlier had played in the quarter final of the British Amateur Championship and a much better player than I would ever be. I thought, 'If I can go to the 14th or 15th hole at least I would not be disgraced — but after four holes played, I was four up — no heroics — just straight pars. Then, I suppose inexperience of that class of golf began to show. I probably tried to preserve my score instead of playing my own game and eventually, I started to lose the odd hole.

I remember it so well — my opponent was two up on the 17th tee and the hole was halved so I lost my one and only county game by two and one. As we walked in, he thanked me for the game and remarked that I had given him a fright early on in the game! — another little memory for a village blacksmith. I also believe I am right in saying that it is or was the only time father and son as players, played in the Shropshire and Hereford County First Team on the same day.

In the early seventies a Shropshire Farmers' Golf Society was formed and this meant more games of golf — more days of matches against different counties — meeting farmers from different areas of the country. How one envied the farmers who did not have that fourteen milkings a week tie. Bob Yates from Shifnal formed our society. He was, at one time, a scratch golfer and played for the county for many years. Many is the laugh we used to have when trying to fit our games in to suit most of us. There was also an Annual Cup to be played for in our own society. The lads in the north of the county, Llanymynech and Oswestry wanted it before they started to hay harvest but that perhaps, did not suit the lads in the south of the county because it could interfere with their potato digging. However, I think those who really wanted to play overcame the various problems — myself included.

Another golf fixture I used to enjoy was the Annual Match against Vicar Cross Golf Club, Chester a — fixture which went on for many years but that fell foul to the change in the drinking laws and as my mind floats back to those days, little incidents keep cropping up like the time about sixteen of us went to play at Sandiway Golf Club. The pro, Tommy Gardiner became a firm friend of mine (as he retired to our village many years ago with his wife, Dorothy). His son is also a professional at Upton Golf Club by Chester. Tommy, now, 78, still plays a regular game of golf. His weight is about ten stones and although he is about 5 feet 6 inches in height, he can still smack a ball about 250 yards with either a bit of draw or fade — whichever he chooses to do — but is a bit suspect on some of his putts. But back to our days of golf at Sandiway. Sitxeen of us from Oswestry went to play and I suppose about seven cars were coming back to the Cross Foxes just outside Overton. Dick Hughes had organised the day out for us and an evening meal at the Cross Foxes. I was with Sam Goff, an older, very keen golfer and he said he knew a short cut back from Sandiway Golf Club to the pub where our meal was booked. The rest of the party elected to follow Sam's car. However, after a few miles, Sam decided that he wanted some petrol and pulled in to a garage forecourt, as did all the other seven or so cars, none of whom wanted petrol. Sam paid for his petrol and drew away, with all the other cars in hot pursuit behind him. I don't know what the look was like on the garage owner's face or what he was saying — not very complimentary, I suppose, after having seven cars on his garage forecourt and only one requiring petrol. It was a good meal, as I remember.

Chapter 46

Caddy and Dad

BY now, Alan, my son, was playing a lot on the amateur circuit — having left school to concentrate on his golf to see how good he could become after a couple of years. He was, a scratch golfer at 17 and the holder of three course records — a 62 at Oswestry, a 68 at Conway and a 72 to equal the amateur course record at the new golf course, The Duke's Course at Woburn in 1976 — a round I remember well because it was in the Prince Charles Trophy for under 18 years of age — one from each county was chosen.

Why I remember it so well is because of two incidents. Alan was not hitting his wood at all well so a decision was made not to carry any woods at all but to use his one iron off the tee on the long holes. With the carrying of no woods, it would eliminate the choice to use them. He played a very good round of golf — 72 gross which won the morning round by two shots from Jeremy Bennet.

On the 17th, quite a high official came up to us and cautioned both Phil Parkin and Alan about slow play. They had, apparently lost a hole on the couple of players in front — fair comment — but they were not holding any other players up. I think at the time, they were a hole and a half up on the players behind them. As we came off the 18th green, this official (I could tell he was an official because he had a blue blazer on with a big badge on the breast pocket) came again to us and had another word about slow play — quite unnecessary, I thought. At that time, I kept quiet.

You could tell by his attitude that he was never wrong so

there was no point in arguing with him. It is surprising what a badge on a blazer can do to some people. However, the story has a sequel. Vera and I had a picnic lunch on the car park at Woburn and by the time that was over, Alan and Phil had started their second round. I caught them up on the third green. They were playing quite quickly. Apparently, the official had had another go at them at the start of their second round — three times he had cautioned them in a matter of a few holes. We were leaving the rest of the field behind. By the time we came to the 15th hole, Alan had dropped about four shots and Phil about the same. Who should be lurking at the back of the tee but the same official. He enquired from me how my son was playing. 'Not very well,' I said to him, 'Thanks to you.' His face went bright red. I said, 'You had no reason to caution them three times, but I will have a word with you when we finish the round.' Alan finished his round with a 77 gross and lost the afternoon round by three shots and the combined morning and afternoon rounds by one shot. By the way, the time taken for the morning round was just over three hours. The official was nowhere to be seen when I was looking for him. Security was very tight due to an IRA scare. Princess Michael of Kent presented the prizes and there amongst the dignitaries, was the official. No way did he want to have a word with a village blacksmith turned caddy for the day.

A few weeks later, I was watching the British Open on television, and in many cases, a five-hour round of golf was the norm. No mention of slow play' so this prompted me to write to the said gentleman to mention that he cautioned Phil Parkin and Alan Strange for slow play a few weeks earlier when they had taken just over three hours for their golf. I received a belated letter back, stating that he could not remember the incident but if he had cautioned them for slow play, he was perfectly in his right to do so — I suppose the blazer with the badge gave him that power and the reason the pros took five hours was that they were professionals and playing for a lot of money — What a load of bunkum!

A game of golf is a game of golf and if you are a professional you should be able to play quicker than the average amateur.

I dropped him another letter, thanking him for his reply but in my second letter, I clearly stated that I totally disagreed with his excuses. He has not found the time to answer that one. I don't think I will ever be on his Christmas card list — he certainly won't be on mine!

Chapter 47

Golfing Ahead

HAVING still a handicap of four, I was chosen as captain of Oswestry Golf Club Second Team to play inter-league matches against other teams in the county. This meant quite a bit of extra work organising and making sure a team of four arrived on the tee at the alloted time. Even if you could not play yourself, the responsibility rested with the captain and as most matches were played on summer evenings, when, in my case, harvesting had to take priority — the old saying 'If work interferes with golf, golf must come first' did not ring true with me. You can play golf in the wet but you cannot harvest hay or corn in the wet — so in my case, priority was kept in perspective — which brings me to one golf match that I will always remember.

I had made arrangements with the captain of Hereford Golf Club to play his team at Oswestry. I was not able to play in the team of four but all went well. The team won their four matches and with a margin of about fourteen holes. The return match at Hereford should have been only a formality — all that was needed was a halved match or not to lose the four games by too great a margin. Somehow or other, I managed to hurt my back through humping bales of hay so I could not play in the return fixture at Hereford the following week but I had to go as non-playing captain as Geoff Roberts and Trevor Edwards were going to be late leaving Oswestry Golf Club. It befell my lot to take Ian James and Peter Barnett who had to be picked up in Shrewsbury from his place of work. I allowed myself about two hours to get to Hereford from Oswestry,

Hereford Golf Club being some seventy odd miles away. On arriving at Hereford, just a bit before six o'clock, I explained to their captain that two of our players would be a little late. We decide that Peter and Ian should start their matches and hopefully, Geoff and Trevor would not be long. Lo and behold, they arrived! Trevor got out of Geoff's car and I could see he was visibly shaking. He said to me, 'I've just got out of a low flying aircraft.'

I said, 'What time did you leave Oswestry?'

'About ten minutes to five,' he replied.

They had travelled seventy miles in just over the hour (no motor way).

Geoff pronounced himself ready and away he went — third player off, leaving Trevor to play at number four. As it was my captain's duty, I went out to meet my team at various holes but sadly, it was not our night. All the first three players through about the seventh hole were one or two down, leaving Trevor quite a way behind them. I walked back a bit to meet him at the sixth green.

'How are you going on?' I enquired.

His remark to me was, 'I'm seven down.'

'Well,' I said, 'you can't be. You've only played six holes.'

'Oh, well, I'm six down,' was his reply.

Trevor was obviously still reliving his car ride from Oswestry. The obvious end to this little golf story is that all four matches were lost and the overall four games went to Hereford by about two or three holes margin. Even today, some fourteen or fifteen years later, Trevor can still remember his ride in, as he put it, 'a low flying aircraft'.

My brother Jack was going to take our heavy farm roller across the main road. 'I'll pop to the top of the Brow Bank to slow the cars down for you.'

But alas, one car did not slow down. It was Geoff. He thought I was waving to him. Missing the three ton roller by a few inches, he sped on his way.

The next time I saw him at the Golf Course, he remarked, 'I thought you were waving at me'. My answer to him was,

'I would have been very annoyed if you had damaged my roller!'

Doug Summerville rang me to ask if I would be in charge of the Shropshire Juniors one evening at Bridgnorth Golf Club. Shropshire Juniors were all fairly low handicap lads from different clubs in the county and matches would be arranged for them against the best players to give them more match experience against good golfers. As I was taking my own son, Alan, also Peter Martin, Alan Lewis and Ian Woosnam (yes, 'young Woosie', as he was then known), I agreed to look after the lads for the evening.

Sandy Lyle and Tony Minshall were also in the Juniors at that time. All the Bridgnorth men were there, except one, and he was to play my son, Alan. He had some problem or other and would be some fifty minutes late. However, we were able to get the rest of the matches away, leaving Alan waiting for his opponent. He arrived some half an hour later and away they went. As was the custom, Bridgnorth were supplying the two teams with supper which this particular night, was a good hot pot — no 'afters' (sweets, etc.) — just one course. All the team knew, except Alan and his partner, who were some forty five minutes late. They went into the dining room for their hot pot, not knowing there were no 'afters'. By now, the time was getting on for ten o'clock. Woosie and the rest of the lads were playing snooker and darts — still no sign of Alan. So I said to young Woosie, 'Go and see what's keeping them.'

After a minute or two, he came out of the dining room laughing. I said, 'What's the matter?'

His answer was, 'They're waiting for their pudding!' No one had thought to tell them there was none.

I am saving a few golf stories for my fourth volume. I think though that I have been one of the lucky golfers, able to afford to play a lot of the championship courses for a few pounds. We used to say with Don Wynn and John Elder that we would have to sell a white faced bull calf to afford two nights at the Forresters, near Bracknell, B and B and evening meal, two days golf at the Berkshire included — today, possibly a two year old Hereford bullock would be required to do the same! But I

menu

Melon

Fillet Sole au Gratin

Roast Beef and Yorkshire Pudding
Roast Potatoes, Garden Peas, Carrots

Fruit Salad and Cream

Coffee

WINES

Château Loudenne
Beaune

have no regrets in taking up that noble game for without it, life would have been a lot duller. Money, as I have said, is not everything. Was it really thirty three years ago that Gerry Williams was captain at Oswestry!

Little did I realise when I sent two Qualifying Cards for the 'Farmer and Stockbreeder' competition at Wentworth what a great day out Vera and I would have. Evening dinner on the top table. Mine all free. Five course dinner for Vera £2.15.0. What price today?

Agricultural Press Limited

161-166 Fleet Street London EC4 Telephone 01-353 5011

A. L. Strange, Esq.,
Brow Farm,
Ellesmere,
Salop.   9th September, 1970

Dear Mr. Strange,

Please find enclosed your starting times and further notes for the final at Wentworth.

I have noted from your recent reply that you would like an extra place at the presentation dinner at Wentworth on Friday, 18th September. To save time on the day, would you please let me have by post your cheque for £2 15s 0d.

Yours sincerely,

S. F. Barrett

164

Broadcasting House,
London.

26th August, 1970

Dear Mr. Strange,

Many congratulations upon qualifying for the Farmer &
Stockbreeder Golf finals to be held at Wentworth next month.

Naturally I consider this achievement should receive
maximum publicity in sporting circles, and would like some
camera shots and location interviews to be shown in a special
edition of 'Grandstand'. I believe Frank Bough comes from
Oswestry which I understand to be your home Club, and I'm
sure Frank will be delighted to present you to the British public
through the medium of television.

What I have in mind is sending David Coleman and/or
Henry Longhurst down to see you, with a team of cameramen,
and you could fill them in on teh background stuff and maybe
show your swing to the cameras. We are negotiating with
Mark McCormack to get Palmer and Jacklin from the States
and if they can get down to Frankton in time we can take
shots of you grouped together as a new Big Three. I feel some
local action stuff, like your carrying your clubs on the muck-
spreader across the main road to the practice ground would go
down well, and also trying to hit drives across Hardwick Pool
(we can bring a load of balls for this purpose).

I would like to make you an offer before ITV see the value
of this homely success story — they would portray you as a
golfing Dan Archer and put you on after the Pig Breeding
programme every Sunday. This, I feel, is not for you, and I
hope you will give your co-operation to the people we shall
send down to Frankton, leaving your fee to be dealt with
afterwards. If convenient J. E. Thomas's will fix a marquee
in the bottom field to accommodate the equipment.

I would be most grateful if, in telling your story, you could
allow Mr. Longhurst and Mr. Coleman to get a few words in
themselves. Again my congratulations.

Your sincerely,
A Fellow Golfer

165

Little did I think when I started playing golf that I would one day play with three winners of the famous American Master's namely Nick Faldo, Sandy Lyle and Ian Woosnam.

I wonder if they realise what an honour it was for them to have played with a village blacksmith.

Chapter 48

Riding School Problems

LITTLE did I think what problems buying a Riding School, ten horses and their stables, saddles and bridles would bring to our busy life-style. We would get to know another, different class of people, the majority of whom were all right but also, some awkward types who would moan, even if everything was fine for them.

The reason I bought out the Riding School was that we had an empty cottage with the old Perthy buildings, as well as some small fields — grand for ponies, with plenty of shelter with big hedges.

My daughter, Valerie was interested in horses at that time. I had unfortunately forgotten the age-old saying, 'Don't expect your children to live your dreams.' Valerie did not show the interest in it that I expected, putting extra strain on Vera — another business to run — more telephone calls, and so on.

Major Halstead, from whom I bought the business, said he would come and work for me and manage the Riding School. This I accepted but within three months, the lure of the Middle East proved too great, and he left to go back to that part of the world — leaving me with the job of finding a replacement at very short notice.

Riding Instructors were hard to find but I think I have said enough about them in my chapter on women and horses. We did manage to survive — with quite a few hiccups on the way. We coped with the extra work for about three years, doing riding holidays for children, as well as letting our cottage for holidays as well — quite a good business — but with quite

167

a lot of hassle, which we did not need at our ages. We made many friends and then, one evening, a phone call from a Lily Morgan gave me a new and different outlook on life. She had been asked by Mrs. Kendall of the Derwen Disabled Workshops and College to form a Riding for the Disabled group of people in North Shropshire and wondered whether we might be able to provide six ponies and two helpers from the stables every Wednesday morning. A price was agreed and that was the start of the R.D.A. in the Ellesmere area — with the help of Mary Clay and a host of lady helpers, too numerous to mention. I think I am right in saying that 1995 will be their 21st Anniversary — and long may they continue. Some of the earlier helpers have sadly, passed on, the majority were already grannies — What a grand sight, overweight grannies tearing round our little paddock holding on tightly to paraplegic children — or leading the ponies. All the ladies' time and effort was given freely and I think that secretly, they enjoyed their Wednesday morning out at Forge Farm Riding Centre.

Soon after we started riding for the disabled, car parking on a Wednesday morning was a bit chaotic with the Smithy customers' cars and also the women helpers' cars. Which brings me to a little story about one of my Smithy customers. He had arrived to have a job done. But alas, nowhere for him to park. He shouted to me from his car, 'Call yourself a Blacksmith with no car park.' He crunched his car into gear and away up the road he went.

I thought I had lost a customer, but after about five minutes he arrived back and came into the Smithy with his welding job and also with the remark, 'I have had to park about 200 yards up the road due to all these other cars about the place'. 'Did you have difficulty in walking the 200 yards', I enquired of him.

'No,' was his reply. 'But what has that got to do with it'.

'Come with me', I said, 'and just have a look what is happening on the Paddock', which he did.

'Now', I said, 'You have children all fit and well, but those children riding on the ponies are all disabled and the cars that were in your way belong to the 12 lady helpers who every

Wednesday morning give up two to three hours of their precious time, so that the disabled students can have the pleasure of riding on a pony. Count your blessing', I said.

He never, ever complained again if he could not get on to the car park.

The Ellesmere branch of the Pony Club go carol-singing every Christmas and have raised over a thousand pounds. Many other organisations have been very kind and contributed to the expenses of the R.D.A. : Ellesmere Round Table, Ladies Circle, Dudleston Heath Gymkhana and of course, the League of Friends of the Derwen, to whom the R.D.A. owe so much.

Horses require feeding, shoeing and with vets' bills so much is needed. Without these organisations, the R.D.A. would not be possible.

Every summer, a picnic ride is organised as a treat for the students. Ponies are hired from Mrs. Peggy Gilchrist and a journey up to the top of the Oswestry Racecourse is the venue. One day there was a calamity. The students were gathered round waiting for the 'goodies' to emerge out of Lily Morgan's car boot — pork pies, sausages on sticks, bread rolls, ice-cream, the lot. But, how do you get into a locked car boot without a key? Not very easily! Everyone was searching, students and helpers would have to go hungry. At last, it was found — in the lock of the car door — the sigh of relief could be heard in Ellesmere and a good time was had by all!

Quite a few of the students had become more confident and were ready for better things so some of them competed in the Open Day for the R.D.A. at Shrewsbury. 'Cowboys and Indians' was their theme and quite a few came home with rosettes — a rewarding day for students and helpers alike.

If anyone would like to help out on Wednesday mornings, they would be more than welcome. So much has been achieved with dedication, patience, hard work, a lot of puffing and an awful lot of laughs. The claim of the helpers is that they have never failed to get a disabled rider on to a horse's back but how true is the tale that they nearly managed once to put a student on a pony facing its tail, I don't know.

One of the horses at the Riding School was a real character

named Hamish. A small Shetland pony, when he thought he had done enough work for the day, he would lie down with the rider still on his back! However, he found his niche and had been trained to pull a small cart fitted with a hydraulic ramp so his disabled owner can get in by himself. Hamish could be seen trotting around the roads of the Wirral with his delighted passenger, Richard Foster.

The decision was taken to sell the Riding School, although at the time, it was being well managed by Susan. Outside influences were 'taking over' — in the form of a party out only for personal financial gain.

What an experience that was — to sell a Riding School, lock, stock and barrel! An advertisement in the 'Horse and Hounds', attracted a lot of attention — but, many people are short of what really matters — collateral.

One instance I recall, of one Sunday afternoon, a lady wasted about four hours of my time. All she did was run down everything she saw, including the house for sale — nothing was right for her. Later, I found that she lived in a rented two bedroomed semi detached house in Salford — with all due respect to those people who lived in semi detached houses in Salford.

From about eighty odd enquiries, a buyer emerged — a lady and her daughter. At this stage, words fail me so I will say no more, in case I am threatened with a libel case. One thing I will say is that she once told me in a temper that she had dealt more in millions of pounds than I had seen hundreds.

'Perhaps you have,' I said, 'but you can't buy common sense no matter how much money you have!'

This proved true as the Forge Riding School was soon up for sale. You don't TELL customers, you ASK them.

The Riding School was bought by Mrs. Carol Perdell, who after many years of hard work, has built up the business again to what it was. She built an Indoor Arena and the R.D.A. have come back after leaving to go elsewhere. The students from the Derwen College put on many displays at diffrent shows and fetes. Every year, they have an annual prize giving and barbecue and two or three have been held at my home, Brow Farm.

170

Competition over the year is very fierce and to win a cup or a shield for the Best Stable Management or Most Improved Rider, brings many a smile to a handicapped rider — who, without the asisstance of the many lady helpers, would not have been able to get on a horse. Long may they continue with more success in the future years.

It was just another little episode in the life of a village blacksmith that reveals another little scene of the kind of village life that sadly is fast diminishing from rural areas — again so terribly English. I do not suppose there are many village blacksmiths who have employed an army Major !

The reason why I have not mentioned many names of the lady helpers with the R.D.A. is that over the past 20 years and more, so many have helped and given their precious time for free that it would require a far bigger book to contain them.

But in mentioning two names at this stage, I convey my admiration of all their work and devotion. The first is Betty Dutton from Old Marton, a farmer's wife, who for many years was the treasurer of the R.D.A. A State Registered Nurse, she attended to the students when they needed medical attention. Sadly, Betty is no longer with us. She passed away a few years ago at no great age. But in her memory an oak first-aid box has been bought and suitably inscribed with her name on a brass plaque. The other lass I name is Frances Johnson, a real stalwart helper, who had the ability to ask people to help with the R.D.A. She could also tell you in what way you could assist as well as make the request, and I can never recall anyone refusing when she was about. Sadly she was killed in a car crash at the age of 45, a death that stunned the whole area, and a terrible loss to the Riding for the Disabled, as Frances was the chairman of the group at the time and doing a great job.

In memory of Frances at the Riding School is a notice board which is used for photographs and news of the group. At the Derewn Training College, suitably inscribed, is a glass trophy case, in which are kept all the awards won each year by the Disabled Riders for their achievements.

The memory of these two stalwarts, and Doreen Hales will

171

live on for many years and I consider it an honour to have been considered as a friend by them.

I thank, very humbly, the many thousands of ladies over the whole country who give willingly of their time to help children less fortunate than their own. Keep going, girls, and long may your Riding for the Disabled continue to bring a smile to a pupil's face that is worth more than a fortune. That says it all.

Chapter 49

Down to Earth. Courting Time

ONE morning, in February, some years ago, I heard terrible screeching in one of our fields. On investigating, I witnessed a scene that possibly not many country people even have ever seen — the start of a courtship between two dog foxes and a vixen. I crept quite close to a gap in the hedge between two fields and about ten yards away were the three foxes.

But what was the screeching every two minutes or so? One fox would come to the gap in the hedge and utter this blood-curdling noise. I could have caught hold of it many times — it was quite oblivious of my presence. (I suppose the smell of animals on my clothing masked my human smell.)

This went on for another few minutes or so, then the vixen decided to lope off elsewhere disappearing over a dip in the ground — to be followed by the two males.

Staying where I was for a few more minutes, hoping to see the foxes again, I was repaid by the re-appearance of the vixen, still followed by her male admirers — all three passed within a foot of me before again, disappearing for the last time over the brow of the hill!

I have told this true country story to many hunting people Not one of them has ever witnessed such a scene, including Sir Watkin Williams Wynn, Master of the Wynnstay Hunt. The sequel, a few months later in our wood, was the appearance of four fox cubs. Many happy moments, Vera and I enjoyed watching them playing around the stump of an old beech tree at the bottom of the field — always at dusk. At the call of their mother, they would disappear into the shelter of the wood. Nature, on one's doorstep.

About two months later, I found two dead fox cubs on the main road passing our farm — run down by the ever increasing speed of traffic. Possibly forty or fifty pheasants and five badgers also perish in this way in the course of a year. With the other predators, young foxes, pheasants and badgers have a very precarious life.

Chapter 50

Anyone for Netball?

VALERIE, my daughter, announced one Friday night that Miss Evans, her P.E. teacher would be calling to pick her up to play netball for the school on Saturday morning at about nine — which brought the remark from me, 'You be ready!'

The picture I had of a P.E. female teacher was of a lady with a manly body, muscle-bound, short hair, ankle socks and tweed skirt!

'You'll like her, Dad,' said Valerie.

'Perhaps I will,' was my reply. 'But you still be ready!' (nine o'clock was about our breakfast time)

Miss Evans arrived on time to be brought into the kitchen by Valerie. What a contrast to the picture I had! Miss Evans was, I suppose, about twenty four years old with a shapely figure, blonde hair — 'A real cracker' as Frank Carson would say. Over the years, I have met Miss Evans (now Mrs. Hughes) many times. She has been to our Smithy demonstrations many times with other pupils.

I recall another incident involving Mrs. Hughes but only as recently as a couple of years ago. The telephone rang and at the other end was a lad named Gregory Baldwin-Davies, asking could he bring about twelve lads and lasses from Lakelands School to visit me at the smithy.

His telephone manner was very polite and a visit was arranged, part of a school project, part of which was to organise the visit to me. I was very impressed by his manner and it proved a great success. The two-hour visit was far too short for me to complete my lecture and demonstration due to the many questions I was asked — quite an interested group. This meant I had to visit the school to finish off the project. After my arrival home, I thought to myself what a nice bunch of children they were, so well mannered and respectful to me, an old village blacksmith. This prompted me to draft a letter to the Headmaster, Mr. Orme, which I believe was read out at morning assembly and also was put on the notice board for all to read.

As with a lot of my stories, there is a sequel — the sequel to this story happened a few months later. With two of my grandchildren, we had gone late-night Christmas shopping in Ellesmere and to see Father Christmas organised by Ellesmere Round Table. Who should I meet but Mrs. Hughes! I thanked her for her letter to me on behalf of the children's visit. Her reply to me was that it was nothing like the letter I had written to the headmaster. She went on to explain what a 'lift' it had given the whole school at a time when the school was facing threatened closure. But the remark she made to me that made me smile was, 'And what a beautiful handwriter you are!' I did not tell her that I am probably one of the worst scribblers in the world. The letter had been drafted by me and Vera, my wife, had copied it out and also forged my signature. I might add that Vera is one of the neatest handwriters there is and to the best of my knowledge, Mrs. Hughes still thinks it was mine. Ah, well, she'll now know different — but Lakelands School is still turning out good, respectful pupils.

Chapter 51

A Blacksmith Remembers

I NEVER thought that one day, I would find myself on picket duty — but as a member of Ellesmere N.F.U., I was requested to go to keep a protest going against the import of Irish cattle at Birkenhead Docks. Why, I have never known but I think it was due to some form of subsidy, Government policy or other. However, I said I would go but as usual, a horse had to be shod before I could go. I took with me Ron Hodnett, Norman Lawrence and Brian Lea.

On arrival at Birkenhead Docks, I went through an open gate and found myself in the middle of the docks. Apparently, we should not have been in there (obviously, a slip up — no one manning the one gate). However, we moved on and could see our other mates manning a picket on the gate with a line of policemen. I wound my window down and shouted to the other lads from Ellesmere, 'Where do you want the heavy gang?'

In no time at all, we were escorted through that gate by two burly policemen and questioned as to how we had got into the docks. We explained our late arrival and what had happened. The police thought that there was no one else to come and the gate we went through in the first place was not needed to be attended. When the Superintendent came we farmers from Ellesmere were summoned to listen to what he had to say. I think there were only eight or ten farmers. I can remember John and Frank Hickson and a Mr. Hughes. The police Superintendent was about six feet four inches tall and wore a peaked cap which made him look even taller. I remember his opening words, 'We will not have any trouble today, lads,' and I think to a man, we all agreed with his remark.

I believe the next day, a much bigger gathering of farmers from Shropshire, some 300 assembled. Our little group was only a token force to keep the television cameras there to keep it in the news!'

There was one amazing incident though I remember when a dear old lady came up to us and said we should 'send 'em all back' — I think she thought we were protesting about immigrants coming into this country. We agreed with her and did not bother to explain that we were protesting about Irish cattle.

Many years ago, I was given some hand bellows, of the small pear shaped type. They were to be found in all Victorian kitchens and often used to get draught into the bottom of the fire. When not in use, they would hang on the wall or by the grate.

As always, my bellows have a story attached to them. They belonged to an old lad who lived in a very old dilapidated country cottage — the roof leaked, window panes were missing and there were cracks and spaces under all the doors. In fact, it was a very draughty old cottage so the tenant decided not to pay more rent until the landlord did some repairs to make it more comfortable. However, the landlord refused and instead got an eviction order against him. The story goes that the two bailiffs arrived at the cottage to serve the eviction papers. They knocked at the door, but received no answer so they decided to push the papers into the space at the bottom of the front door.

To their dismay, they found the papers being blown out again. Apparently, Charlie was sitting the other side of the door, using his bellows to blow the papers back. After several attempts at the front door, the two bailiffs decided to try the back door.

Charlie heard them and quickly nipped through the kitchen into the back kitchen. I am told the space under the back door was even bigger than that under the front door. Out came the eviction papers and out came the bellows — the same procedure followed — as fast as the bailiffs tried to push the papers under the back door, Charlie blew them back out again.

The story goes that one bailiff was heard to say to the other, 'I'm buggered if I'd pay any rent living in a draughty old hole like this!' It is a story I never tire of telling . . .

Taking my son, Alan, one evening to a Wrexham football match, (one of the player's names was Billy Ashcroft) and as usual, Alan went down to the touch line to sit on the wall with the other youngsters. When he came to me at half time higher up in the paddock, he said to me that Billy Ashcroft's mother was standing behind him. I said, 'How do you know that?' His reply was that she kept on saying when Billy Ashcroft had the ball, 'Come on, our Billy!' — Get your facts right . . .

Many years ago, Frankton Cricket Club ran a weekly Bingo evening which eventually attracted a lot of people and what started as a small weekly session soon became big business. Buses from Oswestry and Ellesmere were commonplace and cars were being parked anywhere. A lot of money was made at that period in Frankton Cricket Club's history. However, the time came when bingo was held every Friday night at 7.30 p.m. with Fred Davies in the shop selling pop and crisps at the interval — a good social night out for all and sundry. But once a year Harvest Festivals are held in our village on a Friday evening.

As brothers Bill and Jack and yours truly were very much involved in the running of bingo, we suggested to other members of the committee that bingo should not be held on the night of the Church Harvest Festival. After some discussion in committee, brother Bill was delegated to go and see the Rev. Castell to find out his views on the rights and wrongs of holding bingo on the same night as the Church Harvest Festival. Rev. Castell's reply was 'Bill, if people want to come to church, they will and if they want to play bingo, they will. It won't bother me.'

The village church and village hall are barely a hundred yards apart. John's field was used as a car park for both. So bingo was held in the village hall on the night of the Harvest Festival .Bill, Jack and I went to church as we have always done over the years and other cricket club members ran the bingo. A few days later, a local farmer came to me in Oswestry

Market and in front of a lot of other farmers, said to me, 'Call yourself a Christian — running bingo the same night as the Church Harvest Festival!' To which, my reply was, 'I never saw you in church last Friday, but I did see my two brothers there.' He murmured some reply about his having to go somewhere else that evening — which brings me to an old saying of my mother's, 'Get your facts right before you open your mouth'.

The two lads who took over my smithy buildings were named Colin Hughes and Harry Dyke. They branched out into making steel buildings, employing a lad, Ash Allum — a right good worker, who could dig a hole or carry a ten feet length of asbestos sheet up any scaffolding or across any plank no matter what height the building was.

Colin Hughes, Ash Allum and Harry Dyke were putting up a steel building just above Oswestry Old Racecourse on a wet Saturday afternoon. Ash was doing his favourite job of digging the holes in which to put the girders.

Offa's Dyke is in the vicinity of this particular farm and a rather sedate couple, attired in walking gear, plus fours, tweeds, the lot. The gentleman went to Ash and enquired the way to Offa's Dyke. Ash's reply was, 'You what?' — to be asked again, 'My good man, can you tell us where Offa's Dyke is, please?'

'No bloody idea,' said Ash. 'Harry Dykes is over there. Go an' ask him!'

In one of my first two books, I mentioned Mrs. Walley, my old Sunday School Teacher, a staunch Congregationalist lady. I also mentioned about her son, Richard, who farmed near Wolverhampton and how he gave me a pound note one Sunday when I was walking as a lad to chapel — he had been recalled to his farm at Wolverhampton and his request was for me to put it in the collection box for him. A little sequel to that happened only a few years ago. I was speaking at Brewood Village Hall to a meeting and in my audience were three or four of Mrs. Walley's grandchildren — one whose name was Tom. He knew the story of the pound note. He did a similar thing — only this time it was a five pound note — which was duly put in the collection!

One customer, Barry Woolham, always liked to get the last day's hunting out of a set of horseshoes, and we used to have a laugh about the thickness of iron left on the shoes. Jokingly I would wear gloves to take the shoes off his horse, saying they were that sharp-edged, I would cut my fingers to the bone if I did not, and I would also claim I had no need to buy a razor blade that week as I would be able to shave with any one of them.

In turn he would inquire whether they would 'remove' the terms used for putting old shoes back on a horse. This was country humour and banter at its best, something that seems to be lacking today as life seems have become more serious.

Chapter 52

Memories

THROUGHOUT my many years as a working blacksmith, most annoying are people who run up a bill, and then ask if they can pay later in the year.

That is annoying enough in itself, but when they leave you to go to another blacksmith to have their work done, then insult is added to injury. Not only do you have an unpaid debt, but you have also lost a customer.

This, I regret to say, has been quite a common occurrence in the horse world. The average blacksmith is usually quite approachable, and if the person in difficulty were to explain his or her situation, a compromise could usually have been worked out.

There is another person who is just as annoying — the one who assures you that a horse is perfectly quiet to shoe, when in fact it is a real bad one. Often you find out much later that the reason the horse was sold in the first place was because of that fault in its make up.

A farrier with a broken leg is no use to anyone. That brings to mind a new customer who had come to live into the area. When he brought his horse to be shod, I had already been warned by him that this particular horse had a bad fault. Very occasionally, it would play up and be very unruly and quite dangerous in fact. When that occurred it was advisable to leave it until another day when he could prove to be perfectly quiet.

However I had succeeded in shoeing that particular horse

six or seven times without bother, something which quite surprised the owner.

As with most of my stories there is a sequel. One evening I went to the farm to shoe him, and, as he did not like being tied up either by a halter or a head collar, his owner was holding his head while I was preparing his feet for the shoes.

Half way through the operation his wife appeared at the stable door with a message that he was wanted urgently on the phone.

He asked if I would be alright on my own for a while, and I replied that as it seemed to be the horse's good day that I would, words which I was soon to rue.

I was about to nail on one of his back shoes when he lashed out with both hind feet, knocking me into the corner of the stable wall, which I hit with great force. I fell back into the corner, winded and for a few seconds could not get up. By this time, he had backed towards me and was lashing out with both hind feet, each foot in turn hitting a different wall, and my head between them in the corner. Had he made contact with my head, it is doubtful whether I would be writing this story.

Luckily I had the presence of mind to roll myself up into a ball, and eventually escaped through the door. Had I attempted to stand up, the horse could have killed me. I was obviously quite shaken, and when the owner returned and asked had I seen a ghost, I was so pale. It took me quite a while to explain what had happened.

I left the horse for that night, but when I went back next night to put the back shoes on, I had no trouble at all. A horse like that one is the most dangerous one has to deal with. Called a 'nutter' in the trade, it is an apt desrciption, for it implies the animal is wrong in the head.

I am reminded of a ditty which advised: 'Beware of the back of a horse and the front of a bull !'

When working on farms from time to time, the blacksmith would always welcome a drink, in my case usually a cup of coffee.

But on one occasion I was at a farm where I knew they were

not all that scrupulous about their hygiene. Added to that was that the maid was not too pretty either.

Over the years, whenever she brought me a drink, I was usually able to dispose of it down the drain. But on this particular occasion, she brought me a drink just as I was leaving, and, naturally enough, stood there waiting for me to drink the contents, to take the empty cup back.

There was no chance of escaping, by pouring it down the drain; she was not going until she had that cup.

I looked at her very ugly face, and also at the contents of the cup, and thinking to myself that she might have been the last to drink out of it, and that it might not have been washed thoroughly since, made my stomach turn.

Then I had a brainwave. I held the cup in my left hand to drink out of it. As I handed it back to her, she remarked: 'Ha Mr. Strange, I didn't know you were left handed like me!'

Peter Done, former Area Manager for Rogers and Jackson, the agricultural machinery specialists in our area, and I were reminiscing over a drink one evening.

He recalled an old lady who lived in this part of Shropshire, who sometimes got her words mixed up and her facts not quite right.

I am led to believe that she liked the odd flutter on the horses and had been given a strong tip for a certain race. Before the race was run, she told a friend that she fancied Bigamy but the friend searched the papers in vain — then found the horse's real name was Big Amy, which duly won.

On another occasion she went to an auction to buy her house. At that time houses were fetching around £10,000 but when asked if she had been successful, she said it had gone too dear.

'How much did it make?' asked her friend.'

'Ten thousand, eleven hundred pounds,' she replied.

184

Chapter 53

Unexpected Answers

WORKING with horses most of the time, it was only natural that I should take my children, Valerie and Alan, to the local racecourse at Bangor on Dee on occasion.

Each would be given half a crown (13p) to put on a horse and we would all go down to the last jump to cheer the horses on, having impressed on the children to remember the number of horse they had backed.

The last jump at Bangor is sometimes the third or fourth on the first time round. One day there was commotion, Alan's horse came over the jump without his jockey on board, having obviously fallen off at the first or second jump. Alan wanted to know why Valerie's horse had a jockey, and his not.

Just you try to explain that to a six-year-old.

As a blacksmith, I have often had to deal with young people, and often they come out with the most unexpected answers.

On a very wet Saturday morning a young lass of about sixteen was booked in for the shoeing of her pony, 10 o'clock was the appointed time. By this time the rain had turned to a torrential downpour.

I thought to myself no chance of the girl arriving, but she did, soaked to the skin.

Taking the pony from her and tying him to the wall, I said to the lass, 'You go into my little shed that I use for an office, strip off and hand me your clothes. I will dry them for you in front of the Smithy fire.'

'I cannot do that', she replied, 'I have got no b . . . . . knickers on'.

185

The look on another chaps' face, who was at that time visiting my Smithy said it all, his eyes popped out and his face went red. I think he thought pornography had arrived at the Perthy Smithy.

Then there was this other young lady who asked quite seriously, as I was shoeing her pony, whether I thought her pony was 'gay'. I ignored the question, pretending that I had not heard her, but after I had completed the job, back she came with the same rather difficult question.

To give myself time to consider my answer, I asked, 'What makes you think your horse is gay?'

'Well,' she said, 'When we go to the Pony Club gymkhanas, he prefers the company of boy ponies to that of girl ponies!'

Arriving at a farm one day, to shoe a pony, I was greeted by the farmer's wife, 'Hurry, please, I need you in the kitchen.'

Hurrying out of my Mini van, I rushed to the kitchen wondering what on earth the problem could be.

She was in a distressed state, asking me to move a big old fashioned sideboard, as her daughter's contact lenses had slipped behind it. The daughter could not see a thing without them and was already late for her music lesson!

In a way it was yet another example of the way the village blacksmith serves his community and the problems with which he has to cope in his everyday life. Somehow he gets to know about human nature in the raw, something I was able to put to good use one day when I was working in the smithy.

Now it is a fact that English people are prone to commenting about the weather. On this very windy day, three men were working just off the Perthy, and at about 1 p.m. I noticed them knocking off for lunch. I knew they would be returning just before two.

The arrival at the smithy of Harry Benson at about a quarter to two, prompted me to remark, 'I'll bet you five bob (25p) that the next three people to pass on bikes will comment on the weather.' His response was intantaneous, 'You're on.'

First past the smithy was Dad, head down, pedalling hard against the wind. 'By gum, it's rough!' he said. One up to Alf.

Next came one of the sons, 'By gum, it's windy!' was his comment. Two up to Alf.

About 100 yards behind, came the second son. 'By gum it's blowing!' he said.

'Pay up, Harry,' I claimed. He thought for a moment then he counter-claimed, 'Bet's off, who are you to believe. One said it's rough, the other said it's windy and the other said it's blowing'. Ah well!

I still have in my possession what we called a grindle stone. About four feet in diameter, made of sandstone, it is used to sharpen the various types of implements used on farms, like scythes, hedging hooks and also axes. It was hard work to turn it on its stand for hours for the sharpening process.

About once every three weeks, Jack and George Morgan, two local timber fellers, (in the days when trees were felled by axe and a cross cut saw) arrived at the smithy.

They would come to the shop in early evening, with a ruck of axes to be sharpened. Jack Haynes, Tom Speke, Ellis Ankers and myself would have the job of turning the stone non-stop for about two hours, and it was always quite hard work for us.

When the axes were all sharpened they would be wrapped in a bit of old sacking as their edges would be razor sharp both to protect the person carrying them and the edge itself.

I remember that occasionally Jack would pretend to have a shave with a newly sharpened axe remarking 'That'll do'. Whehter he actually ever had a shave with it, I do not know but the childhood memory of his action is as vivid today as it ever was. I remember we lads would be given about two-pence between us for the night's work and it would not last long for Pat King's shop would be open until around 9 o'clock for us to spend our hard-earned pennies.

One of my favourite customers was Peter Ward, one of whose hobbies was brewing his own ale! If you arrived at dinner time his first remark would be 'Bar's Open'. And the same greeting would meet one at six o'clock at night!

Peter was the only man I know who could make a horseshoe, never having had any formal training in the art. He built his own blacksmith's shop complete with hearth and anvil. This man of many talents had, I believe, also built a church organ. Peter served in Bomber Command throughout World War Two.

One farmer for whom I worked always reminded me of a job I did not do for him. Apparently, he brought me a set of harrows for sharpening one Saturday and wanted them sharpened by Monday morning — a physical impossibility. Every time I met him subsequently he told me that he'd had to sharpen them himself.

Now that incident happened at least 45 years ago and I had not seen him for a long time until I happened to bump into him a couple of years ago.

True to his nature, he brought out the old story of the harrows. I thought to myself that it was a great shame he had nothing better to think about. But why bother, I thought, it takes all sorts! He himself never married and when I go and see my grandchildren playing football, I know full well who is the happier.

During my long career as a blacksmith, I became acquainted with a quite famous football manager. At the time, I was friendly with an old gentleman who had been a supporter of that particular team, man and boy for 40 odd years.

One day, I thought as a special treat to him, I would ask that manager whether I could bring the old gentleman to the club, maybe meet a couple of players, and perhaps stroll to the centre circle on the ground. It would have been a tremendous treat for an aged old lad.

Fortunately I did not tell him what I had in mind but approached the manager first, asking him whether he could arrange such an outing.

I received the curtest of replies, 'No chance', was the message as he gave me the impression that I should have gone on my hands and knees to him.

However a few weeks later in the company of two of my mates, both professional men, one remarked on what a wonderful half day they had had with their sons at this particular club. The manager had taken them to see the players training; they had met the players in the dressing room and it had been a real treat for them and their children.

I have not had the pleasure of telling that particular manager what I think of him but if he reads this, he will know who he is. It does not matter now as my old mate has gone to pastures new.

In fact the manager himself was relieved of his post shortly afterwards which reminds me of the old country saying, 'Be nice to people on your way up as you might meet them on your way down.

Countryside characters are full of old sayings like that which are both witty and wise and all too often show accurate observations of human nature.

Some I have heard include: A man who was going bald was having his leg pulled by his mates. His response, 'You have to scrape the hair off a pig'. Another couple of sayings are, 'Look towards the sun and the shadows fall behind you'; 'It is only dead fish that swim WITH the tide'.

Letters

JUST a couple of letters out of many I have received in the past few years.

Great Shepcraft Farm,
Stretton,
Warrington

7.12.88

Dear Alf,

I have just finished reading the two books you have written and published, a friend lent me them in the summer and I waited for the winter evenings plus the fireside before the opportunity of reading them came my way.

What a wonderful story you have given to your readers, so well written with such talent, you certainly are a prince of story tellers. To those of us who lived through the times and experienced the way of life you have described, your stories come to life. While reading the stories, many times I would start to chuckle, and then read the stories to my wife, I always believe a good thing, it is always better shared. Both my wife and I come from farming families, so many of the stories are applicable to growing up in farming families. I left school in 1927, worked for my father till 1942. My wife and I started farming in 1942 on our own, and are still able to carry on enjoying life on the farm. My work is with the dairy cows, I still enjoy milking cows, my son who farms on his own, looks after the arable and feeding cattle on this farm as well, our two daughters are married to farmers and take a keen interest in farming. I am one of four brtohers, my eldest brother who lives in Anglesey and still does a little stockfarming, I feel he would greatly enjoy reading your books, so I am enclosing a cheque for £7, I hope this will cover cost of books and postage, I should be very pleased if you could autograph them. I once listened to Alastair Cook reading his lettter from America, telling the story of two refugees from Hungary who made good in America, he finished his story and then made the comment *'It all happened in our Time'*.

I am,

Yours sincerely,

Alan Richardson

Henlle,
Whittington,
Oswestry

7.1.84

Dear Mr. Strange,

I have newly read your book about life at Perthy between the wars. I would like very much to thank you for taking time to write down your memories. It would be a tragedy for such pleasant memories to be forgotten.

Naturally it was of great interest to me as I knew some of the characters one cannot help but wonder how much life has changed in a short period.

The Lord moves in a mysterious way. I wonder if this book would have been completed but for your illness.

I feel most grateful that you published this picture of rural life for future generations.

I deriveated great pleasure from reading this book.

Also thank you for your interest and care of young people.

Yours sincerely,

D. J. Ellis

Chapter 54

Favourite Story

MY favourite story, which happened just before my enforced retirement, concerns an eleven year old girl named Sophie, who lived about three miles from our smithy at Dudleston Heath.

I was shoeing her pony when she appeared on the yard in quite a distressed state and really crying. There was no way I could pacify her but after about three or four minutes or so, after my many questions as to why she was crying, she blurted out, 'Oh dear, Alf, I'm in terrible trouble. I have failed my 11+ exam.'

I stopped shoeing her pony and put my arm around her and said, 'Don't cry, Sophie. It's not the end of the world failing your 11+.'

In this particular case, it was, as she had an elder brother and two older sisters who had gone on to further education, and here was she, the youngest, failing her 11+.

I sat her down on my shoeing box and said to her, 'Look, Sophie — I failed all my exams at school, left at fourteen and I have made a living shoeing horses. You don't need education to make a living — just common sense and you'll get by.'

I can see her face even now. It will always be with me, as well as her remark through her tears, 'Yes,' she said, 'Mummy says that all I will be good for will be to help Alf Strange, the blacksmith.'

I'll add no more to that story, only to say that children always speak their mind. A lot more children stories will appear in my fourth book, I promise.

On a tomb stone in Oxford is the inscription :
> 'Under this sod, lies another'.

My tomb stone will bear the inscription :
> 'Here lies an honest blacksmith'.

— in years to come, people will say, 'Well isn't that STRANGE?'